THE BALLOON BUSTER

With their observation balloons calling the shots, German artillery was ripping the Allied army to shreds. Yet to destroy them, an Allied flyer had to blast his way through a squadron of enemy fighters, and then descend into an inferno of flaming shrapnel from innumerable antiaircraft batteries and long-range machine guns. To most Allied flyers, balloons were sheer suicide. But to Frank Luke, Jr. they were a golden opportunity, a heaven-sent shortcut to glory and fame. In seventeen blazing days, he destroyed more enemy balloons than any other flyer in World War I, and set a standard of heroism and deadly skill that has never been surpassed.

THE BALLOON
BUSTER

NORMAN S. HALL

THE BALLOON BUSTER
A Bantam Book / published August 1966

Library of Congress Catalog Card Number: 66-22420

Published simultaneously in the United States and Canada

Bantam Books are published in Canada by Bantam Books
of Canada, Ltd., registered user of the trademarks con-
sisting of the word Bantam and the portrayal of a bantam.

PRINTED IN CANADA

Bantam Books of Canada Ltd.
156 Front Street West, Toronto 1, Canada

THE BALLOON BUSTER

I

HIS name was Frank Luke, Jr.

He was as arrogant as Lucifer and as direct and straight-forward as a boy. He was as self-centered as a motion-picture star, yet he once stumbled twenty miles through the Arizona desert into a town, then back to the sand and cactus, saving his last quarter so a crippled friend could eat.

In his high school days he liked to masquerade as a girl, yet he could wade into a mining-camp dance-hall crowd and smash belligerent ore handlers into submissive silence.

He could step into the saddle at dawn and stay with it until sundown—today, tomorrow, and the day after that. Day upon day he toted a seventy-pound pack over the buttes and rim rocks of the White, the Hieroglyphic, and the Superstition mountains with the sure-footed tirelessness of the mountain sheep he stalked.

He worked in the copper mines of Ajo shoulder to shoulder with veteran rock men who had gutted the hills from Chihuahua to the Coeur d'Alene, and when he needed extra money he gave dancing lessons at night.

He could put a rifle bullet through a daisy as far as that flower is recognizable. He could do more tricks with a six-shooter than a monkey can with a coconut; but when he fought, he fought with his hands—cleanly, victoriously, and with a smile on his face.

He collected tarantulas and German machine guns,

1

motherless lambs and fatherless French children. His closest male friends were a hunchback and a famous aviator. He saved the hunchback's life. He led the flier to his death.

In many respects he was the greatest military aviator the world has known, yet his commanding officer described him as "the damnedest nuisance that ever stepped upon a flying field."

He was awarded the Congressional Medal of Honor, but if he had lived he would have been recommended for a general court-martial.

He spat at the stars and grinned because it was good to be alive; but at twenty-one, with an opportunity to surrender honorably and live, he crouched over an automatic pistol, kept it smoking until the hammer fell flatly on the empty clip, laughed at the gray troops hemming him in, and crumpled and died.

The world had gone to war. Within four phases of the moon men donned earth-brown clothing that did not fit, grasped rifles that were awkward and strange to their hands, and slogged off across the world—mighty and proud in the newly gathered knowledge that a wrenching twist would free a rib-held bayonet.

They became drunk with wine and high resolve and fear and the sense of their own importance in the new raw, red scheme of existence. With glamour and with gold they bought women who, had they continued to walk in normal ways, would have been as unattainable as the stars.

Some, content with this, stood afar off, did nothing, lived, and were raised to high places; others accomplished the impossible and were battered into the mud of a foreign field for their pains.

Of the latter was Frank Luke, Jr.

Not always do "the paths of glory lead but to the grave." Too frequently they begin where a stone marks the resting place of a corpse.

It was so with Luke. Since that September day in 1918 when a terse War Department regretfully informed his parents that he was missing in action, a thousand orators have

2

voiced his praise, a hundred writers have clicked out fragments of the saga of "the brave, mad flier of Arizona."

But the only speeches he ever heard usually began with: "Why the hell is it you are the only man who finds the regulations of the United States Army too irksome to live up to?" And any writing connected with his name was apt to take the form of a squadron memorandum confining him to ground duty because of some breach of discipline.

Not that discipline annoyed him. He didn't treat it seriously enough to allow it to become an annoyance. He ignored it. Yet he ruled his intimates with an iron hand.

The kids he ran with were always known as "Luke's Bunch," never as "Pinney's Crowd," or "Elder's Gang," or "Akers' Mob"; although when it came to concerted, whole-souled hell-raising, "Pidge" Pinney and Bill Elder and Johnny Akers were certain to be found just beyond the smoke and flame.

It mattered little whether it was a fishing expedition to the junction of the Salt and Gila rivers, or a football game with the Mission Indians—who understood a good deal about kicking but relatively little concerning football—Luke led. He assumed leadership as his natural prerogative, and until the day of his death found willing followers.

Arrogant? Self-assertive? Beyond question; but it was a wide-grinned arrogance, a smiling self-assertiveness, that created a desire to follow him. He was at his best when the odds were against him; triumphant when it seemed he could not win.

What a leader for a forlorn hope in the old days! Given a regiment, a broken sword, and a bad moment for his side, and Frank Luke, Jr., could have held any hill until the guns came up.

He looked the part, too. At sixteen he was man-size: stood five feet ten inches tall, and weighed 170 hard pounds—hard as an ebony block. His shoulders were the envy of every athlete in the state. Had you gone into Arizona a few years after his death and asked the football crowd if they had known Frank Luke, they would have responded:

"Know Luke? You betcha! The toughest line plunger in Arizona."

His was a long face characterized by straight lines: a straight nose; a straight slit for a mouth; gray eyes that gazed straight at one, questioning nothing, volunteering nothing, apparently waiting for the one on whom he gazed to make the next move.

He smiled at the slightest provocation, and it must have been a winning smile, because even those who knew him only casually remembered it years afterward. It touched his mouth, his eyes, and, as Bill Elder described it to me, "You gathered that he was glad to just be there and walk around and say 'hello' to folks."

He had a moderately high forehead topped by thick, straight blond hair—blond as a canary's wings. It was a good-looking ensemble, even handsome, and the most pronounced characteristic was the chin. The man—the leading, scrapping, chance-taking male—showed there. It suggested but one thing—courage.

His father probably gave him that, for in the eyes of Frank Luke's dad flickered the fires of fine, high courage. Not the flashing, spectacular bravery of his war-bird son, but the determination to overcome obstacles, no matter how great; a determination all pioneers must possess if they are to survive, and the Lukes were pioneers.

The elder Luke came to the United States in 1866, six years after his father emigrated from Dahlhausen, a small village in the province of Westphalia, Prussia, near the Holland border. The flier's grandfather, after serving a year in the Union Army during the Civil War, established himself in New York City and gathered his family about him. It was during this period that he altered the spelling of his last name from Lüke to its English form.

Several years later a brother who had been serving as a commissioner representing Arizona in Vienna, Austria, returned to the United States and took Luke's father from New York to Arizona with him.

They arrived in Prescott in April, 1873, and the aviator's father resided there until 1877, when he received an appointment to the United States Military Academy at West Point. Failing to enter because of defective vision, he returned to Arizona and took up his residence in Globe, then a rapidly expanding mining camp.

Mr. Luke dabbled in mining activities, but disappointment over his thwarted military career chilled whatever ardor he may have had for the work. He was an enthusiastic hunter, and countless times gunned for rabbits over the ground where the mighty workings of the Miami and the Inspiration copper mines sprawled fifty years later. In 1880 these properties were considered worthless; by the 1920's they had earned $75,000,000.

In the latter part of 1880 he went to Phoenix, then a sun-baked frontier town of less than 1,500 inhabitants. There he met the woman who became his wife. Her family had emigrated from Berlin several years before and had come to Phoenix in 1879.

Shortly thereafter Mr. Luke became politically active and held a number of offices. In the 1920's he was a member of the Arizona State Tax Commission.

To Mr. and Mrs. Luke nine children were born: Eva, who married former United States Attorney Thomas Flynn; Anna, who became Mrs. John Sherry; Edwin, Charles, Otilla, who married Eben Perry; Frank, Regina, who married Edward Wilson; and John.

Frank was the odd one. That seems to have been definitely established May 19, 1897, when a lusty wail announced his presence. His father declares that, as a baby, he yelled a little louder, kicked a little harder, and ate with greater gusto than the others.

Funny, how there usually is one in a family who is geared a little higher than the rest, and who keeps his nose a trifle farther out in the breeze. The nose gets whapped occasionally, but the owner does go places, meet people, and see things.

Frank Luke, Jr., had that kind of nose.

You could tell his brothers that something out of the ordinary was taking place around the corner and, when they had finished the job in hand, they'd stroll around to look it over. Not Frank! As soon as he gathered that the occurrence was outside the usual routine, he was high-tailing it in the general direction of the excitement.

As a small boy he was an amazingly jumbled mixture of cherub and spike-tailed devil. At the age of four his hands had been slapped, the seat of his trousers dusted, and innumerable paternal frowns bestowed upon him because of unauthorized sorties into the surrounding countryside.

But these disciplinary measures were treated with the disdain he later displayed toward the regulatory measures of military superiors.

He had exhausted the possibilities of the yard, and the interior of the barn was as familiar as the palm of his hand. There must be new worlds for this Alexander. Outside the gate lay the open road, and strange territory was just beyond the first thank-you-ma'am. He sallied forth.

Mid-afternoon and naptime came, but no inquisitive head was poked from the last place imaginable in answer to Mrs. Luke's call. Mild surprise deepened into anxiety, and when a thorough, frantic search of the grounds and outbuildings produced no Frank, there was consternation.

The sun slipped behind Squaw Peak and neighbors were making their second sympathetic inquiries, when a moving blur down the road focused attention. It moved falteringly, wearily, and, finally aware of the women scampering toward it, sat down heavily in the middle of the road.

With a sobbing cry Mrs. Luke scooped the bedraggled figure to her breast. As she did so, a woolly ball rolled from beneath each of the child's arms and plumped into the dust. Slowly the balls unwound into fuzzy animals.

"What," gasped Mrs. Luke, "have you there?"

Frank wriggled to the ground and possessed himself of the weak-legged creatures.

"Sheeps," he announced proudly. "Two sheeps. Man said if I could carry 'em I could have 'em."

It seems that a considerable distance along the road over which he had adventured there was a sheep ranch. The owner, observing the youngster intently watching several lambs feeding, had offered as many of the animals as Frank could carry away.

That night there was some talk of corporal punishment, but Mr. Luke vetoed it.

"Any youngster of mine," he declared emphatically,

6

"who shows that much interest in dumb animals doesn't get punished for it, and that's that."

Not long thereafter, however, Mr. Luke altered this tolerant attitude toward the collection of Arizona fauna. Following the episode of the sheep it was considered advisable to keep a closer check on Frank's activities. In due time this duty fell to his sister Otilla, and it was observed that the system worked marvelously.

To be sure, there were many mysterious trips to the open country, and the Indian kitchen servants reported innumerable requests for empty tin cans, but no importance was attached to either.

Then Mr. Luke decided to go fishing. Being an ardent and a successful fisherman, his requirements were simple but well founded in tradition.

One of his needs was a can for bait, but it must be the proper sort of can. Fortune is much more apt to smile upon the angler who goes equipped with a vegetable can still retaining the jagged lid. The jagged lid serves excellently as a handle and adds a spicy note of danger in that it is certain to gouge deeply into a thumb before the day is over.

In search of such a receptacle, Mr. Luke entered the barn. His eyes glowed with satisfaction as he saw a row of about twenty cans neatly arranged on a crossbeam. He grasped one and pried up the lid to assure himself that it was sufficiently clean to receive his garden worms.

Immediately thereafter he fetched a whoop that awoke vague memories in the breasts of the red-skinned kitchen help, flung the can from him, broke the standing-broad-jump record, and grasped a spade.

With the air of a man intent upon the business in hand, he smartly bashed a large tarantula. He lifted his second can and there followed another whoop, a new broad-jump record, and further activity with the spade. The can had contained another tarantula.

One of Mr. Luke's characteristics was his mild demeanor. He was a devout man who used profanity sparingly and, except in moments of great stress, never in the presence of ladies and children. But by the time the fifteenth can had yielded the fifteenth tarantula, Mr. Luke's temper snapped.

"How," he demanded, with certain trimmings I shall omit, "did these qualified tarantulas get in here?"

He addressed himself to his wide-eyed family, who had been brought to the barn door by the erratic but sustained thumping of the spade.

He received his answer from the least expected source.

"Tilla," a piping voice wailed, "dad's killed our bugs!"

Frank, newly arrived on the scene, had taken in the situation at a glance.

"Did you put those da—da—dangerous things in here?" his father demanded.

The big toe of Frank's right foot traced a perfect square in the dust as he replied, "Uh-huh. Tilla and me was collecting 'em to get a hundred."

Mr. Luke looked warily behind him before continuing the investigation.

"What, in heaven's name, did you want with a hundred tarantulas?" he asked.

"Aw, just to get a hundred," said Frank, and Tilla nodded solemnly as though the amassing of a hundred deadly tarantulas was one of the goals of life.

Mr. Luke did go fishing that day, but he carried his worms in a paper bag.

In his sister Tilla, Frank found an adventurous spirit much to his liking. She even was permitted a part in the game of Soldier, and this game lay very close to young Luke's heart. True, she usually was cast as the enemy, but it is remarkable that her brother permitted any girl to participate, for in his early youth Frank Luke, Jr., was decidedly a man's man.

The childhood game of Soldier is as old as the spirit of strife; it probably will survive until the end. You will find it played in the roaring heart of New York's slums. Go among the squalid villages along Central America's Mosquito Coast, and you will see the revolutionary armies of tomorrow drilling, marching, charging—and always to victory! Who dares say that one of these armies of childhood ever retreated?

8

But, as Frank Luke played it, it was a rugged pastime. No field-force commander threatened with defeat at the hands of the enemy and mutiny in his own ranks ever directed the activities of his troops with the hawklike vigilance Luke displayed. To soldier under him was to be a veteran indeed.

He knew that some peculiar, unexplainable gesture of fate had deprived his father of a military career. But was he not his father's son? And what did fate have to do with it, anyway? Let fate wait a while, for there were mightier forces to be reckoned with!

The blonde head of the enemy—Tilla—could be seen around the corner of the barn, and Frank Luke and two neighboring kids and a scampering puppy would run that enemy screeching and panting right up to the kitchen door.

Tiring of the din of battle, he sought quieter ways. Pidge Pinney helped him find them.

Albert C. Pinney at that stage of his career was round and inclined to leisure. In fact, Pidge was something of a promoter. Years later he assisted his father in the management of the largest exclusively sporting-goods store in Phoenix and became one of the best-known sportsmen in Arizona.

Pidge suggested a collection of birds' eggs. "You take birds' eggs, now, Frank," he urged. "We'll get a walloping collection of 'em and maybe we can sell 'em."

Frank's eyes glowed. This was something like! You had all the fun of playing, and you were enriching your earthly store at the same time.

The birds'-egg collection began that afternoon.

Then Frank met Bill Elder. There are few friendships such as that one: the sort of man-to-man liking that causes you to feel strangely alone when in the presence of one who has participated in it. The type of falsehood-free regard that sends men rolling down the avenues of fame or faltering to the gallows' foot together.

It began in a sun-washed Arizona road when two barefoot kids looked upon each other for the first time. It ended when Frank Luke squeezed the trigger on his last cartridge and pitched forward across the bullet-pocked fuselage of his plane.

Ended? No, I don't mean that. When I talked with Bill Elder, I knew that friendship would not end until Bill Elder bumped off too. And, so long as we've got to believe in something, let's believe it won't end then.

Elder's people came to Phoenix shortly after the San Francisco earthquake.

Frank and Bill met in the road and circled each other warily. Bill, who had big-city brashness, spoke first: "Hullo."

"Hullo."

"You live around here?"

"Uh-huh; in that big house."

"Bill's my name. What's yours?"

"Frank. I'm named after my dad, Frank Luke. Where d'you live?"

"Right down there. We came from Frisco."

During the remainder of the morning the traveler who actually had seen Frisco talked and Frank listened. When the latter hopped off to a belated lunch he was convinced that his morning's acquaintance was either the most marvelous liar in Arizona or the best scout in the world. It wasn't long before Frank decided he was the best scout in the world.

Luke, always aggressive in defense of his own rights and those of his friends, was particularly so whenever Bill Elder was concerned. Although Bill was a hunchback, he needed no special rules in any man's game. But Frank Luke big-brothered him nevertheless.

Elder had a natural reserve which added mightily to his personality and I do not believe Luke ever fully fathomed it. Even in the barefoot stage Bill would pause to estimate the situation; Frank would plunge in: characteristics that risked and saved Elder's life in the years to follow.

On one occasion when Frank had invited Bill to remain at the Luke home for dinner, Elder seemed reluctant to take his seat at the table.

Frank pushed him forward, but his chum still held back, explaining in a whisper: "Your pop looks cross."

Frank cast a glance at the amply surrounded table, directed a quick, straight look at his father, then spoke:

10

"Aw, sit down. Dad's got so many of his own he won't even know you're here."

Through the years Bill was the strategist; Frank the hard-boiled field commander. Early in their friendship they discovered that their homes cramped their styles hopelessly, so they moved into a tent in Frank's yard. Pidge Pinney was declared in and contributed many entertaining, if somewhat devastating, ideas.

There were some who said that there wasn't a farmer or a rancher in the Salt River Valley who wouldn't cheerfully have returned to the era of six-shooter law rather than see the trio descend upon his holdings. But mostly they just chuckled, and years later voiced a wish that they could go back to those days and have the triumvirate with them again.

Wise farmers who raised melons gave them an item in their overhead. Those lacking in wisdom kept vigil with the moon and a shotgun in one patch while the three were raiding another.

They hunted incessantly, and anything that walked on four legs, or crawled, or had wings, was game. Had any earth-swooping angel suddenly become visible to them, it would have been a tough break for the angel.

Once, this penchant for taking a snap shot at anything that grew wings proved to be a tough break for Frank. It also marked the only time Bill Elder saw him frightened. I have been unable to find anyone else who ever saw him scared.

Frank and Bill were returning from a hunting trip and Frank deftly placed a .45-caliber bullet through the neck of a chicken. They drew it, and were watching it come to a golden brown over a small fire of mesquite, when they were joined by a middle-aged stranger who held serious conversation with them relative to the ownership of the fowl.

Both immediately admitted they had bought the chicken that morning, but had delayed the cooking until after sundown. Unconvinced but powerless to act in the face of this argument, the chicken rancher retired.

The boys ate leisurely, resaddled, and headed toward Phoenix.

They had jogged along a few hundred yards when Frank

11

started another chicken and promptly drilled it. The smoke was still drifting lazily from the muzzle of his six-shooter when a flat, hard voice at the roadside snapped their heads about.

"You assorted so-and-so's, get down off them horses," it said, and the two hit the road in a hurry. It wasn't the voice so much as the single-action .45 the owner of the voice held waist-high. He was the conversational chicken rancher who had visited them at their fire.

"I've watched ya," he informed them, "and followed ya, and now I've got ya. You"—he indicated Elder with the gun muzzle—"kin git. But this chicken-shootin' friend o' yourn is goin' to stay."

As Bill Elder told it to me:

"I slid up into the saddle while the old fellow walked out and took Frank's gun away. He sure was mad, so mad it struck me funny until I looked at Frank's face. He was white, and I could see the muscles stand out along his jaw. I knew he was scared, and I also knew if Frank was scared there wasn't anything funny about it. Boy, I sure high-tailed it for Phoenix.

The chicken rancher marched Luke to his house, from which a tow-headed youngster took a message to the sheriff's office. The tow-head's entrance to the peace officer's sanctum, as later described by that official, would have been good for any second-act curtain.

"My pop's got the feller that's been shootin' his stock," he bleated.

Now, a chicken rancher may, if he so desires, refer to his chickens as "stock"; but in Arizona, even today, "stock" is usually construed as meaning cattle.

The sheriff blinked and took both feet off his desk. Somebody been shooting cattle, eh? Wel-l-l-l! He shifted a six-shooter from his hip pocket to the waistband of his pants, let his vest fall over the butt, and stepped to the inner office where several deputies sat.

"You boys better come with me," he said meaningly; adding, "And come heeled."

They went. At the ranch they found a white-faced youngster sitting opposite a frontier-model .45 behind which

12

crouched the chicken rancher. Upon a near-by table was a grisly corpse of a chicken.

I can find no record of the case from then on, but the popular version is that a disgusted sheriff turned a white-faced youngster loose with the muttered hope that there would be a returning and more dead chickens.

Luke unquestionably was frightened, but the scare did not affect his other activities—particularly football. Every autumn Luke's Bunch played the Indians at St. John's Mission. The games were interminable. They began as soon after breakfast as sufficient players for two teams could be assembled. They ended when the contestants were too bruised to continue, or because of darkness.

As football it was an atrocity, but as a workout for sprouty young cubs it couldn't have been bettered.

The Indians favored discarding the ball entirely, for they regarded it as a nuisance that deprived one of their number of the use of his arms. The palefaces played with the spirit that characterized plainsmen in the days of the pony express. As a matter of fact, these encounters failed of a place in history merely because gunpowder wasn't used.

Luke liked football. Given the ball, he would line-plunge a barbed-wire fence. I've talked with some of the Indians who played against him, and they encompassed a world of things with their laconic "You couldn't stop him."

He broke an arm in one of those games and was carrying it in a sling when the old Central School opened for the fall semester. For some flagrant breach of discipline he was summoned to Principal Randall's office and sternly informed that he was to be flogged.

Flogged?

Young, gray eyes—hard now—lifted in a straight gaze into the professionally frowning ones of the school head.

Flogged!

A white spot in each cheek where the jaw muscles were bunched tight.

Flogged!

A straight slit of a mouth biting off words:

"You won't flog me!"

Luke wheeled, stepped past the astonished principal, and

strode to the stairhead. He glanced back, saw that Randall was following, poised for an instant, and deliberately— *jumped!* He hit halfway down, cradled his smashed arm with his good one, and rolled to the bottom. Randall, aghast at the boy's act, dashed after him. They met at the foot of the stairs, and again the lad spat:

"You won't flog me!"

Randall didn't.

II

THE Arizona heat made a corrugated cooking vessel of the arroyo-slashed desert land rimmed by the naked buttes. Upon their broiling tops a copper-hued sky with a burning knob of sun for a handle fitted with suffocating snugness. Saguaro cactus drowsed in the yellow glare like gaunt, misshapen creatures from another world.

Silence—the dead, flat silence that breeds in heat—possessed the land so thoroughly that even the desert reptiles respected it and remained still.

But to Frank Luke and Bill Elder, riding slowly toward the somber foothills of the Superstition Mountains, the baking wasteland was a refreshing and invigorating place.

Since the previous September they had been cramped and stifled in cool classrooms. There had been recitations, examinations, and a hundred and one other activities invented by parents and educators to make the winter months unbearable.

To be sure, there was next year and high school, but now they could stretch and be at their ease.

Suppose the saddle horn did get so hot you carefully avoided touching it? What if smarting rills of sweat did run down into your eyes? Any guy who didn't get a kick out of these things would suck eggs, and if he wouldn't suck eggs he would fight, and if he wouldn't fight he was beneath contempt.

As they plodded along, a buzzard sideslipped into their

range of vision, leveled off, and executed a perfect falling leaf into a deep arroyo, then gathered air speed and made altitude again. Luke slid a rifle from a carbine boot, cocked the hammer, and cast an appraising eye at the looping, soaring scavenger.

"Can I get him?" he asked Elder.

Bill eased over on the near side of his saddle and grinned. He knew Frank's ability with a rifle.

"Ought to be easy," he said.

Three times the sights lined up on the winging black body aloft. Three times Luke held his fire. Finally he slapped the rifle back into the scabbard and hooked his pony.

"Aw, let him go," he said. "He isn't harming us."

Less than five years later this little episode was to be recast, with Luke in the bird's rôle. It was Luke who side-slipped and soared and maneuvered into falling leaves.

Below him, the hunters were lining up their sights—but when they had them trained on him they did not let him go. They brought him down as a wounded eagle comes down—in a sweeping rush—and, like the eagle, he fought them even then. Grounded, his wings crippled, he clawed savagely with the flaming talons modern warfare had fitted to his hands.

Thus did greatness come to him.

In the early days, when he thrilled to desert heat and mountain cold, there seemed little of distinction in this let's-take-today-to-hell-with-tomorrow youngster. Except for name and physical characteristics, he was no whit different from many other hard-fisted sons of the Southwest.

Red-faced generals and bull-voiced orators would have been forced to draw heavily upon their imagination to make of him a figure about whom they could build their empty phrases.

Here it should be recorded that Frank Luke had promised himself greatness. Death snuffed him out before he had decided what particular field of endeavor was to know his name, but the desire for conquest was strong within him and he frequently discussed it with Elder.

At night, over their lone red spot of fire in the blackness of the Arizona hills, they talked of many things, these two, and largely of themselves. Squatted on his haunches in the fire circle, Bill would ask:

"What're you going to do when school's over, Frank?"

And the prompt answer:

"I dunno—yet. But it'll be something good. You wait and see, Bill."

A solemn nod from the squatting Elder. He would wait and he would see, for he had never known this partner of his to cover too much territory. Whatever Luke said he would do he did. He was everlastingly on the long end of things, too.

Once, when returning from a hunting expedition, they camped on the desert twenty miles outside of Mesa, a Mormon settlement fifteen miles from Phoenix. Made careless by fatigue, they did not picket their animals—two saddle horses and a pair of burros. When they rolled out at sunup their stock was gone.

Frank cut for sign and satisfied himself that the two saddle horses and one burro had gone toward Mesa. The other burro had strayed back into the desert.

Frank imparted this information to Bill and they grinned sheepishly at one another. They had curtailed their hunt because the pack grub had been exhausted, and the last of their game had been consumed at breakfast the day before. The strayed mounts meant that a square meal was still many hot hours away.

Bill would have favored a thorough discussion of the situation, but Frank ordered immediate action. Luke knew his native country sufficiently well to realize that the lone burro would not stray far into the desert, and that the other three might amble to Mesa or on into Phoenix. He dispatched Elder after the desert wanderer, while he scuffed away over the sandy trail left by the others.

Within an hour Bill caught up with the burro, roped him, returned to camp, tightened his belt, and prayed for rain.

Doggedly Luke plodded along the twisting trail of the runaways. By 10 o'clock the sun on his back no longer burned. It had become a dull, red pain. Arizonians will tell you the desert sun at noon is hotter than at mid-morning. That isn't so. It couldn't be. It just seems hotter.

Frank's gun belt galled him, and when he attempted to shift it the cartridges in the loops stung his hands. He wondered vaguely why they didn't explode.

The sun climbed higher and, for the first time, Frank realized that a force you cannot see can hit you a definite blow.

He thought of the desert as an oven and his imagination brought him the tantalizing odors of his mother's kitchen. He sniffed hungrily and cursed—a thing he seldom did.

Ever before him lay the tracks of the animals he followed—two big ones and a little one; two saddle horses and a burro. He mumbled it over and over again until it became a kind of chant timing his footsteps:

"Two big ones and a little one; two saddle horses and a burro."

Twilight had painted cool blue shadows on the desert when he came upon the animals at the edge of the irrigated country just outside of Mesa. They recognized him and, as though remorseful for the trek they had caused, trotted in his direction whinnying.

Too trailworn to vent his anger on them, Luke improvised halters with the lariat he had brought from the desert camp, swung astride his own mount, and rode into town.

Now he could eat!

At the first lunchroom he dismounted and strode eagerly to the door. But he did not enter. Withdrawing his hand from the doorknob, he slowly sank it into the pocket of his Levi's and as slowly withdrew it, seemingly reluctant to gaze upon what he knew it would contain.

A lone twenty-five-cent piece!

The odor of food filled his nostrils. His eyes, bloodshot from the merciless glare on the desert, rested on pastry, neatly piled. He hadn't eaten in two days, and at that time twenty-five cents would buy a substantial portion of food in an Arizona lunch room.

But that two-bit piece was the sum of Luke's and

Elder's cash, and Bill Elder, who also hadn't eaten in two days, was twenty miles back in the desert.

Again Frank mounted his horse—more wearily this time—and headed back into the arid land. He admitted to Bill later that he had thought of buying food and bringing it back with him, but had not dared trust himself to carry it.

To attempt a credit arrangement with the lunchroom proprietor did not occur to him, and that was very characteristic of Frank Luke. He would pay his way or fight his way, but no step of any way his feet ever trod was paid for by begging.

When Frank arrived at the desert camp, Elder was asleep. Frank packed the burros, policed the camp litter, saddled up, and then awakened him.

"Come on, Bill, let's go," he said. "I'm hungry.

Nor was this the only occasion when Frank Luke disregarded his own well-being for the comfort and safety of Bill Elder. Under his leadership they often found themselves in the swirling, tumbling vortex of a man-size jam.

Under the same direction they rode through to safety, not infrequently with the lean, hard hands of disaster clutching at their stirrup leathers; and invariably Luke was carrying the heavier portion of the load. This because of desire rather than necessity. He gloried in the knowledge that he withstood more of the rough going than the other fellow.

About a year after the episode of the strayed horses and the two-bit piece, Luke and Elder arrived at the White River Indian Agency to find the river in spate. The usually sluggish stream had become a writhing, rumbling monster that chewed out great bites of clay bank and swept away tough-rooted mesquite and cat's-claw trees.

A roving band of Navaho Indians was camped at the ford a short distance below the agency buildings. The young bucks—hardy swimmers all, to whom a swollen mountain stream was but a rugged incident in the day's journey—had counseled caution and urged their elders to pitch tepees and wait for the river to subside.

To this group of desert rovers Luke announced his

intention to cross the river. One—a heavy-shouldered, box-faced Indian, whose skin bulged with folds of hard muscle—gave the slim white youths cool appraisal, glanced at the swirling water, and shook his head.

"Not good," he said; then returned to the group at a small greasewood fire and sat down heavily. If these striplings wished to proceed despite a wise man's warning, let them.

Elder waited patiently for the orders he knew would be forthcoming. After carefully scanning both banks, Frank spoke.

"I'll go first with the burros," he said. Then, as an extra safeguard for his less hardy friend, he added: "And wait until I ride out on the other side. Understand, Bill?"

"Uh-huh," Bill grunted, and wondered what would happen if one of those tossing mesquite stumps hit you when you were in midstream.

He soon knew what would happen!

Luke urged his horse into the shallow shore eddies, the reluctant burros strung out behind on a long lead rope. When the water was stirrup deep, a sharp hook from Frank's spurs sent his mount lunging into the boiling yellow flood.

The Indians scrambled up and moved to the river's edge for vantage points from which to view the contest. A man and a horse against the elements! This was familiar strife worthy of their critical attention.

With spur and hand Frank tooled his pony in a diagonal course for the opposite shore, giving low-voiced encouragement the while:

"Steady, girl, steady! 'At's the stuff! Take it straight on. Easy, now, easy."

He had weathered the sweeping current and his horse was shouldering up the steep shale bottom on the far side when one of the burros behind him floundered, fouled the lead rope, and, with a squealing, bleating grunt, rolled under.

Realizing that he might lose the pack animals and be dragged in himself, Luke lifted his horse in a rearing circle that landed him in deep water again, brought his sheath

20

knife down in a flashing full-armed swing, and severed the lead rope.

The heavily burdened burro rolled up, was caught by the current, and swept downstream. A few moments later Frank's tired pony was straining up the bank.

Luke dismounted, emptied the water from his boots, and bawled encouragement to Elder.

"All right, kid," he shouted. "Let 'er buck!"

Frank turned to tighten a latigo strap. A moment later he was charging along the bank, seeking a spot from which a long jump would carry him farthest into the turbulent river.

A saddle-colored Indian brat, naked as desert rim rocks, saw the danger first. As he emitted a shrill howl of warning, a thickly branched mesquite stump, borne swiftly on a yellow-lipped wave, smashed Bill's horse in the near fore shoulder, unseating the rider. The stump swung end for end and Bill grasped it.

He was dimly conscious of a faint hail from the far shore: "Hold it, Bill! I'm comin'!"

Your Navaho expends his emotions frugally, but as Luke's lean body slashed the yellow water the Indians growled their approval.

Could he make it, this gold-haired one? Could the little one withstand the buffetings of that mad, twisting beast in its trough below them? The old, old struggle. Man pitting his naked hands against the forces the Great Spirit had made before he thought of man!

Luke's head and shoulders heaved above the surface, his arms swinging in a rapidly timed trudgen. Perhaps it is the way Indians cheer a man who is waging a game fight; perhaps something in the measured rise and fall of the river battler's arms was reminiscent of the beater-stick's fall on the tom-tom head; at any rate, they urged him on with a rhythmic:

"Hi yah! Hi yah! Hi yah!"

Elder, now hopelessly entangled in the mesquite branches, had not seen Frank enter the water. He was struggling futilely to free himself, his strength failing rapidly. He rolled, sucked in a mighty mouthful of dirty yellow water, and kicked himself to the surface again. Another one like that would—

Something had him by the hair and he was being half washed, half dragged across the swirling current. He felt gravel crunch beneath his feet and lurched out of the water. He was conscious of cheering at a distance, and a familiar voice was saying:

"Take it easy till you get your wind, Bill." And then, "Say, those Indians sure can holler when they want to, can't they?"

Elder rested, while Luke transferred much of the load from the remaining burro to his own mount. When both had dried out, Bill crawled to the pack animal and they headed for Roosevelt Dam.

Elder, shaken and spent from his experience, rode in silence, the sullen roar of the river still echoing in his ears. He wanted to shape his gratitude in words, but could not make a beginning.

It is difficult to thank a man for saving your life when he jogs along whistling, one foot thrown over the saddle horn.

Late that afternoon they rode up to a small group gathered about a deep pool at the foot of Roosevelt Dam. Serious attitudes and low voices spoke eloquently of tragedy. A woman who lived over yonder. Fought a lot with her husband. Yes, it might be suicide. Drowned about an hour ago.

There was something in that word "drowned" Elder did not like. He moved away from the knot of people, but not before he heard Frank inquire:

"Anybody tried to get her?"

A stocky man gave drawling answer: "Ain't nobody dared, I reckon."

Luke regarded the men with cool contempt and spoke with quiet scorn.

"It doesn't seem as though you could all be yellow," he declared. In a surprised silence, during which there was no attempt to resent his insult, Frank stripped and walked to the edge of the pool.

"Watch my duds, Bill," he called, and dived.

For two hours he plumbed the icy depths of that spring-fed pool in a courageous but vain effort to locate the body.

Between dives, he conversed only with Elder. By the words of their spokesman, the others gathered there had withheld a service because it was arduous and distasteful. With such Luke had no desire to mingle. Defeat he could understand; but reluctance to engage in any competition that might result in defeat was beyond his comprehension.

Particularly was this attitude evident in the future ace's career in school athletics. Many, many times as a track man, when captain of the Phoenix high school football team or as a leader in scholastic baseball, he knew that he and his team were going in against men they could not best.

But Frank Luke fought as cheerfully and as aggressively under the drab standard of defeat as he did under the gay colors of victory.

With him a game was never ended until the final whistle blew. No matter what lead his team might have, Luke wanted more, and drove them in to bring it back to him.

Studies he clung to less tenaciously. Work—hard work of any description, whereby some tangible result took shape under his eyes—he enjoyed. He deliberately selected a man's job and was openly proud of his ability to achieve a man's share of credit.

During several summer vacations he worked in the New Cornelia copper mine in Ajo, one of the largest and most famous copper properties in the world.

Accompanied by a chum, Floyd Craver, Luke journeyed first to the mining settlement a few days after he completed his sophomore year in high school. The youths were offered positions as truck drivers. Craver accepted, but this was something less than Frank had anticipated. He had informed his cronies in Phoenix that he was going to Ajo to become a miner, and a miner he would be.

His shift boss was openly skeptical. A man had to have more than a good-natured grin, an arrogant eye, and a schoolgirl's complexion to make his mark with the New Cornelia gang. But he put Luke on.

The shift received him without comment. Hammerfisted old-timers for the most part, they had learned the folly of snap judgment. Sometimes these pretty boys could go, and go plenty. Not infrequently a level gray eye was the badge of the killer, and Messrs. Colt and Smith and Wesson had reduced mankind to a plane of amazing equality.

Luke worked. Within a week he was setting the pace for the shift, and this was as unwelcome as it was unexpected. So long as veterans in any field of endeavor can maintain their superiority, they do not resent the presence of a youngster or two. But let the youngsters draw ahead and tolerance sours to disfavor and open hostility.

Nor was the disfavor with which Luke was regarded in any way relieved by his willingness to discuss his prowess at all times and with all comers.

The older rock men hit a comfortable stride and watched grimly. They knew what was coming and they dreaded it. A mine-level row is nasty enough when confined to two men; but when a shift divides against itself, it becomes a roaring, blood-flecked melee that fills mine-company hospitals and populates mine-settlement cemeteries.

Luke's shift was about evenly divided.

Frank worked and talked. He moved about Ajo blissfully unconscious of whispered comments and covert identifications—unaware that the toughest jam he yet had experienced was slowly shaping itself in the echoing, smelly tunnels of the New Cornelia.

It came swiftly, as those things do.

A knot-headed little Irishman named Breen, unfriendly since Luke's first day in the workings, selected the mid-afternoon slack period as best for his purpose.

As Luke, carrying a heavy bundle of short drills, strode down the level, Breen so timed a backward step that Frank could not fail to collide with him. The two bodies met, Luke's drills clanking to the rock floor. Breen's snarl rose above the clatter.

"What the hell is the matter with you?" he barked. "Need this whole mine to walk in?"

Although surprised, Frank saw the battle light in Breen's eyes and sensed the Irishman's purpose. Taking a short step forward so that the fallen drills would not trip him, he eyed Breen steadily.

"If I do," he said, "I'll take it!"

They started punches almost simultaneously, Luke's blow landing squarely as Breen's swing glanced harmlessly off his shoulder.

Unconsciously the miners separated into two groups: Breen backed by his adherents, Luke clustered about by those who had placed a mental bet on him.

And the kid could go!

He smashed a long, straight right that brought blood and splintered teeth from Breen's mouth; followed it with a short, jolting left to the wind, then a one-two to the head— hard, deftly placed punches that hurt.

Like almost every rough-and-tumble fight ever waged, the first blow decided it—that smashing right to Breen's head. The squat Irishman, battle-schooled in the cantinas of Northern Mexico and the mining-camp barrooms of Arizona and Colorado, had planned that punch for his own. It was to have been a jaw-crunching blow that would have humbled this arrogant blond upstart he thoroughly disliked.

But now Breen was blocking, ducking, weaving, striving desperately to avoid flailing punches that added mightily to his hatred and his pain.

And what a setting! Uncertain yellow light thrown upon tensed figures—grotesque, shadow-shrouded. Pockets of light and shade in the uneven walls. A litter of tools on the floor, over which the two straining antagonists struggled and separated and hit, clinched and broke and struck!

Jumbled voices. Flat, cold curses of satisfaction. Quick, hot whispers of warning. Breen, whose code countenanced a hobnailed heel in the mouth if his opponent went down. Luke, who smiled and stepped back when Breen stumbled. But it was Luke who had Breen on the wall when the shift boss descended upon them in a bellowing charge and broke it up.

Of Frank, unmistakably the victor, the foreman demanded explanation.

"He asked for it," Luke said through punch-thickened lips, "and I gave it to him."

25

Then he remembered the group behind Breen and added, "I'm not looking for trouble, but if there's anybody else in this bunch that wants some they can step out!"

He ran his eyes over the men nearest him, to find them all intent upon the business of mining. Lustily the shift boss cursed him back to his job; then he curtly ordered Breen to the surface.

Turning, to find Frank bent over the fallen drills, the foreman chuckled.

By God, they were still breeding men in Arizona!

III

WHEN the adolescent male becomes concerned with the crease in his trousers, when a soft if slightly frayed collar no longer is preferable to a stiff new one, when he does not have to be reminded that his hair needs trimming, *cherchez la femme!*

This—like a changing voice, the down before the first shave, and an Adam's apple out of drawing—is a very necessary stage in attaining man's estate.

It requires the addition of a new nail file to the household toilet equipment, increases the consumption of face powder —heretofore regarded with mild disdain as a weakness of mere woman—and usually brings to the face of the sufferer a calf-eyed expression of moonlike simplicity for which the sane members of the family would cheerfully boot him.

He begins to be misunderstood, life is hard, and—some day—he will go away and Forget!

In the majority of cases it attains its most virulent stage about the sophomore year in high school, and Frank Luke, Jr., was no exception. Heretofore Frank had regarded all girls with tolerant superiority. He liked having sisters—a fellow could borrow a dollar occasionally and he knew that some of the bunch had a lot of fun with the girls at school, but he—Well, he was a man's man.

What a bubble that was!

I am not in a position to record here the name of the girl who pricked it, but it is remembered that some fair Arizonian was sufficiently rash to remark that she thought

Frank Luke was actually handsome and that she was "cra-a-zy" about the way he looked in football clothes.

The symptoms recounted in the opening paragraphs of this chapter became apparent immediately after that bit of information reached Luke's ears.

He was good-looking, and the tales of his football prowess, Bill Elder's rescue, and his victorious clash with Breen did him no harm in feminine eyes.

Frank soon became as competent in a parlor scrimmage as he was on the enemy's ten-yard line with three minutes to play. He became the catch of the season and saw to it that he frequently was caught. He was an excellent dancer and, during the ensuing school vacation, used this knowledge to advantage.

With Floyd Craver he returned to Ajo and his work in the New Cornelia mine, but found it less profitable than he deserved. On borrowed money, Luke and Craver opened a dance hall, where Frank further improved the financial situation by giving dancing lessons to ore-footed miners.

In moments of stress he doubled as his own bouncer, and not a few boisterous mine hands learned that he possessed a pair of hard fists as nimble as his feet. The Breen story had spread and it was not long before he and Craver were conducting the most orderly place of entertainment in Ajo.

Arrived, then, Battling Haney of Frisco.

The Battler's advent at Ajo was one result of a visit paid the mining town by a third-rate fight promoter, who saw in the thriving settlement a profitable field for his activities. In the privacy of his favorite back room he explained the situation to Haney somewhat in this manner:

"It's velvet, Bat. Even a mug like you can walk away with a lot of them pick-swingin' monkeys' dough. We'll go down there an' offer to match you with the local punch t'rowers an' clean up."

Haney wrinkled a low forehead in what passed for thought.

"Yeah," he said dubiously. "But suppose one of them guys is good?"

The promoter sneered: "Ya can take it, can't cha?"

The Battler nodded. Indeed, his claim to fistic fame was based solely on his ability to "take it."

There were permanent ridges along the Haney jaws raised by having the Haney head repeatedly wedged between the foot rail and the bar; but Mr. Haney was remarkable in that he always extricated the head in time to drop his antagonist with a deftly placed "sucker's shot" driven from behind.

In the ring he was more careful. He regarded any blow below the knees as foul, no matter who hit it.

Upon the arrival of Mr. Haney and his manager, Ajo went into executive session to decide upon a fitting opponent. There was a Polack who ran a hoist in B shaft who was pretty good, but a rigger had whipped him, and Breen had slapped the rigger into a pensive mood.

Breen, it was recalled, had been punched out of shape by that blond kid from Phoenix; the smiling young chap who ran the dance hall. A delegation waited upon Frank.

Would he meet Battling Haney of Frisco in a six-round bout?

Frank demurred, citing his lack of ring experience; but when he was informed that the fair name of Ajo would be forever smirched if Haney returned to the Coast without having encountered an opponent, he smilingly agreed to do whatever the boys wanted. Then he promptly forgot the engagement.

The night of the fight he was patiently saying, "One, two, three, step; one, two three, slide," to a pair of animated violin cases on the ends of a miner's legs when Floyd Craver rushed in.

"They're waiting for you, Frank," he panted. "The hall is full and Haney's ready to go into the ring."

"Be with you in a minute," Luke replied. "Just as soon as I change my dancing shoes."

With this message Craver sped to the scene of the fight, repeating it to the waiting Haney and his manager.

"Wot ta hell?" queried the latter. "Who is this guy?"

"He gives dancing lessons," a hanger-on informed him.

A slow grin spread over the manager's face, a satisfied smirk that was mirrored on Haney's battered countenance. A dancing teacher? Geez! Were these tunnel rats goofy to

29

give Battling Haney a set-up like that? A dancing teacher! Geez!

Haney entered the ring first, a professional scowl clouding his swart features as he scanned the packed, eager audience. There was nothing new in all this to him. Strange faces about him and a new arrangement of lights, that was all.

He had gazed upon the same thing countless times before in Wyoming and Nevada cow towns, in Colorado and New Mexico mining camps, in border come-on settlements, flaunting their exaggerated vice for wide-eyed tourists. Suckers all. He liked suckers. They bet their money and he dropped their favorite. A sweet system.

Applause and spoken encouragement mildly rippling along one aisle marked Luke's progress toward the ring where Haney, his eyes screwed into a calculating squint, waited. The Frisco boxer had had Ajo's defender pointed out to him, but this was his first close glimpse.

He regarded the white skin, the carefully combed blond hair, the good-natured grin—then angled five words out of the corner of his mouth to his manager:

"Watch me take this baby!"

Luke gave serious attention while the referee instructed them, but he was smiling again when the gong sounded and he stepped out quickly to meet Haney.

It was fast enough—on one side—for even a mining-camp fight audience. Scarcely had the gloves touched when Luke was drenched with a rain of punches. The driven leather smacked on his eyes, his cheeks, his mouth, and painted red blotches on his white body.

The crowd roared its mingled glee and blood lust in a raucous, pride-humbling guffaw: a guffaw that cost Haney his easy Ajo money.

For a fleeting instant Luke saw himself as the crowd saw him—inept, inferior, easily bested by a third-rate gin-mill pugilist. Frank Luke, who ever prided himself on being as good or better than the other fellow at anything he elected to do, going down to inglorious defeat in the first round while the crowd laughed!

And on a day not long gone by he had thrashed the best one of them—Breen!

Why, they pointed him out on the street! Spoke of him as "That kid Luke, a bad boy to stir up," and were proud of him! He had a place here, had earned it, and this mauler from the Coast was making him a laughingstock, a clown, in the eyes of men who, a few minutes before, had respected him! What had he to be proud of now?

This!

This one straight driving right to Haney's chin that, for the space of a heartbeat, stood clearly etched through the blur of gloves!

The blow went home and the smashing impact of it stilled the crowd. Haney swayed, a gray film grew over his eyes, and he sprawled to the canvas.

Not until the referee's arm had fallen in the final count and he was reaching for Luke's right hand to hold it aloft was the silence broken.

The first sound, a wail, came from Haney's corner in the voice of a man who realizes that the impossible has overtaken him:

"Godalmighty! The Battler's *out!*"

Followed a rafter-shaking roar of approval that heated Luke's cheeks. His pride was well bolstered now!

Not long after Luke's one-round victory, Floyd Craver was killed in a truck accident, a tragedy that had a sobering effect on Frank. Loyalty to friends was one of Luke's strong characteristics and he had been particularly fond of Floyd. The latter's end marked the first time death had interfered with his plans, and this dulled the edge of things for many months.

Later he was to experience again that sense of loss, poignantly, bitterly, when Lieutenant Joe Wehner—at the time almost his only intimate in the squadron—did not return from a dogfight. There was another, Lieutenant Roberts. But much remains to be told before I write of them.

In the fall Luke closed the Ajo dance hall to return to his studies in the Phoenix High School and his place in the backfield of the football team. To him the gridiron was, by far, the most important feature of the curriculum. He trained for it, too.

Frank's sister Tilla once commented on the fact that, unlike most of his classmates, he did not smoke.

"I'll tell you, Tilla," he explained. "I like to do things, and to do things you gotta be in good shape. Smoking might spoil my wind or something, so I don't smoke."

A touch of the Spartan there. Frank Luke wanted the pinnacles, but he was willing to climb for them and he didn't grouse if the going was rough.

He was all for the team, too; willing to work for the privilege of playing, and whenever there was any advertising to be done Luke took a leading part.

His favorite stunt was to masquerade as a girl, which he did with remarkable ability, and, accompanied by several teammates, to clown about the streets of Phoenix, thereby starting an informal parade that ended at the playing field.

Tiring of this method of exploitation, Frank turned to bigger and better things. To Bill Elder, Pidge Pinney, Perry Casey, and a few other cronies he confided his scheme. A parachute jump! At noon, after his aides had engaged in the proper ballyhoo, Frank would jump from the top of the new high school building with a large wagon umbrella for a parachute.

There were mild protests, but Frank waved them aside. Were the protestants going to heel on him, or would they be regular eggs and promote the proposition? All voted the regular-egg ticket.

The first farmer encountered who had his wagon umbrella not bolted to the wagon body contributed the parachute and Luke's aides spread the news:

"Be at the high school at noon tomorrow!"

The resultant crowd was all that even the promoter of the stunt could have asked. But he forgot to consider school officials and certain other sane citizens who had reason to believe that such a leap might do more than advertise a coming football contest.

Accompanied by admiring friends, Frank ascended to the roof of the high school building, and was making ready for his spectacular jump when a self-appointed vigilance committee arrived and almost forcibly terminated the exhibition.

32

As a compromise, the wagon umbrella was permitted to float ungainly to earth, carrying with it a burden of old clothes. But, until the day Frank Luke actually took the air as a war bird, he declared that he had been cheated of a new and thrilling experience.

Frank's next public appearance was at the Junior-Senior class pennant rush, during which he collected a nickname, innumerable bruises, and the whole-souled wrath of every peace officer in Phoenix.

The pennant rush—still a feature of Phoenix high school life—is a good, old-fashioned head-socking, eye-gouging contest which has for its object the hoisting of a class pennant to the top of the school flagpole. It's fun. So is an Irish riot!

It was a Roman holiday for Luke. In the early stages of the brawl he was clawed so free of clothing as to be thereafter spoken of as "B. V. D." Luke. The bruises came as the clothing went. The wrath of the peace officers did not materialize until the gloaming.

That year the Seniors won. That is, they succeeded in hoisting their pennant to the flagpole's top.

Late that day, armed with a Colt .45 and aided by the dusk, Frank crept to the foot of the pole, took careful aim, and shattered the brass ball atop the slender shaft, as well as the twilight peace of Phoenix, with six rapid shots.

Six-shooters that hadn't been drawn in months flashed from holsters, as police, deputy sheriffs, and marshals converged toward the scene of the shooting, each running peace-upholder dreading to be the first to stumble over the bodies.

The shooter was gone. The pennant wasn't. Muttering words all policemen seem to know, the officers returned to the places from whence the fusillade had drawn them and arranged their corns in comfortable positions. But not for long.

What Frank Luke couldn't accomplish with a .45 he could with a beloved twenty-gauge shotgun he possessed. His quitting the flagpole was in no way occasioned by reluctance to meet the law. It was because he recognized in the shotgun a superior weapon and had sprinted home to obtain it.

Two reports—in the evening quiet they sounded like a battery of seventy-fives getting under way—again filled the streets with the pound of heavy feet. Surely, thought the charging badge-wearers, there must be a Mexican rebel army around that flagpole this time!

There wasn't. Just a blond Junior critically examining the remnants of a Senior pennant lying at his feet.

What did they do? Well, what would you have done?

When Frank became a Senior it occurred to him that the lives of freshmen were much too placid for such hapless creatures, and he took immediate steps to remedy the situation.

"Bring me," he instructed his cohorts, "some freshmen."

Several first-year men, bleating mildly and struggling mightily, were led before the Master Mind, temporarily ensconced behind a signboard at a prominent street corner.

After a preparatory cuff or two, the hair of the sacrifices was clipped and their heads shaved. Following brief instruction in the deference due a Senior, the freshmen were released.

A harmless prank, were it not for the fact that several of the boys whose heads had been shaved were, in the idiom of Mr. George Ade, Prominent People.

From their parents came a protest loud and sustained, which resulted in the expulsion from school of Luke, Bill Elder, Perry Casey, and one or two others involved in the hazing.

But Luke also was Prominent People.

Even then Phoenix was proud of him. He regarded life with a friendly grin that usually evoked a similar response; but when it scowled in return, he reached out and hit on the button—hard!

In him resided aggressive courage and good-natured contempt for authority.

Adobe might crumble to make way for modern office buildings, flivvers might park at curbs where paint horses once dozed at hitching racks, but so long as there were Frank Lukes the old Southwest still lived.

Arizonians smile encouragingly on such men.

34

Overnight Frank's escapade—no one even thought of attributing the leadership to any other member of the group—was the principal topic of conversation.

Almost without exception the action of the school authorities was condemned in terms sometimes indelicate and always emphatic. Frank Luke a menace to discipline and respect for authority? Nonsense! A malicious mischief-maker? Foolishness! Just a grinning young hellion. An easy-going buckaroo of whom great things would come one day.

That day then was speeding to its wrath-red dawning. A day when all America turned to its easy-going buckaroos, its grinning young hellions, and asked their all.

They gave it—dear, just God, *how* they gave in a thousand stinking, corpse-strewn dugouts; in forgotten towns; in lousy, blood-wet trenches foul with the very odor of death; in wood and wheat field, farm and fen.

Hellions? Look up at the roof over your head and give thanks because they *were* hellions! And one of the best, Frank Luke, a grinning hellion until that last, mad, flame-swept moment beside his battered plane!

So strong was public sentiment in favor of Frank and his friends that Dean Scarlett of the Trinity Episcopal Cathedral in Phoenix and Dwight B. Heard, publisher of the *Arizona Republican* and one of the state's wealthiest men, personally waited upon the school authorities and had the expulsion order withdrawn.

Luke expressed his gratitude as only he could.

In the next football game, against Flagstaff, he sustained a broken collar bone in the first period, refused to leave the field, and, with one throbbing arm dangling uselessly, slammed his way through a tough defense for a touchdown.

If you could only have a Frank Luke with you when a jam started!

For a game or two Luke played brilliant football. Pidge Pinney was in at quarter and Perry Casey was playing end. Being cronies, they delighted in making plays together, and, when all else failed, Pidge would whip the ball to Frank for a muscle-tearing line plunge and gains.

It didn't last long, however. Frank broke training and was temporarily suspended from the team.

This gave him more leisure than he was accustomed to—a situation that could have resulted in almost anything. It did bring about another clash with the authorities.

Frank suddenly became aware of the great number of red lanterns nightly displayed about building operations, and decided forthwith that a collection of these warning beacons would be interesting.

With two companions, he set out to assemble the lanterns in one spot, and so enthusiastically had he discussed the project that the three vied with each other for the record bag of lights.

Soon after the hunt began the sheriff's office temporarily abandoned all other activity in Phoenix and turned to the apprehension of the lantern thieves. The law triumphed and the lantern collectors were provided with a cell each in the Phoenix lockup.

Believing that an hour or two of confinement was sufficient punishment to discourage any future sorties of like nature, the sheriff released them.

Frank's companions faded quickly from the scene, but Frank was detained in the sheriff's office by his older brother Edwin, then serving as a deputy.

Ed was a little fed up with Frank's escapades and spoke forcefully.

"Dad will skin you," he said, "and mother will worry her head off if you keep this up."

There was more, much more, in similar vein until Ed, believing Frank entirely chastened, paused to let him speak.

"Aw, listen, Ed," said Frank plaintively. "What're you hollering about? Why, you ought to be proud of me. Didn't I get the most lanterns?"

IV

TIMED with the measured thud—thud—thud—thud of an
ax sinking into seasoned timber, a resonant young voice
chanted:

> Foot—foot—foot—foot—sloggin' over Africa—
> (Boots—boots—boots—boots—movin' up and down
>   again!)
> There's no discharge in the war!

The cadenced ax blows and the voice came from the yard
in the rear of the Luke home, and Bill Elder, who had ap-
proached the side gate unheeded, laughed. He had heard
this marching song of Kipling's many, many times, for it
was Frank Luke's favorite, invariably used as an accom-
paniment to any physical activity which lent itself to rhythmic performance.

Miss Sarah Whitfield of the Phoenix High School faculty
had taught Frank the verse, which he would recite at the
drop of a hat—yes, even without this formality. He had a
way of rolling out the stanza-ending line,

> There's no discharge in the war!

as though it had some deep significance.

Who will say it didn't? For the only discharge he was

to know was written in rifle fire at the edge of a shattered wood.

That war, in which there was to be no discharge, was upon him even then. It was Bill Elder's first topic as he sauntered to the woodpile where Frank worked.

"I've just been reading the bulletins down at the *Republican*," he said, "and it looks like we'll be in this European fight before we know it."

Frank sank the ax in a convenient block and nodded slowly.

"Maybe," he agreed doubtfully. The war was vague, distant, impersonal. Europe and France, Verdun and Murvaux, still were only colored sections and circled dots on maps, interesting him so little that he immediately fell to discussing plans for a hunting expedition he and Bill were to embark on the following morning.

In the cool quiet of early evening five days later they rode into the mining town of Globe, east of Phoenix. It was a momentous day, but to Luke and Elder, jogging slowly over the barren hills, nothing had occurred to make this April 6 in any way different from others they had experienced.

On the outskirts of the straggling settlement they passed a white house—neat, inconspicuous enough, but famed to everyone who knew Globe because of the business conducted therein. From a second-story window an American flag, limp in the still air, hung flat against the twilight blue.

Flags fly but seldom from the dwellings of those who seek the night and greet the day with drawn blinds. There was something startlingly incongruous in its presence there, and something oddly humorous too, that drew a jest from the dusty riders.

They passed groups of miners who conversed intently, a new seriousness marking them. Women clustered at fences and talked in low tones.

"Maybe somebody's been hurt," offered Bill, for it was that kind of setting.

Luke remained silent as they rounded a corner into the full blare of Globe's Tenderloin. Every nickel piano was at its tinkling noisiest at a time when the town usually relaxed in its last few minutes of quiet before the night's carouse.

Here was animation, a new quick, high-pitched enthusiasm that explained itself to Luke and Elder in snatches of conversation from knots of voluble, gesticulating miners on the sidewalks. The sober-heads had gone quickly, silently to their homes to discuss the awesome news with their women.

In town, where the material for toasts was ready to hand, the hot-heads had gathered to have their say and boast and mouth threats.

A drunken Serb raised his voice to describe what would happen to "that—— —— —— —— of a Kaiser now!" and cheered his fatherland. Not far distant a group of Australians gazed on him in surly silence.

A motorcycle in front of the telegraph office pop-popped into life and roared up the hill to the mine superintendent's home, where the executive awaited the orders the rider bore.

Double production in the mines! Copper and more copper for shells and the breech facings of field pieces!

War! Patriotism!

A drunken peasant, who remembered his homeland only as a place of squalor and poverty and oppression, cheering a king he never saw . . .

Enmities, hatreds, born in a chance word on the street . . .

Worried young husbands talking in twilight peace of death to come . . .

A flag flying from a brothel!

Until the dawn, the smoke-wreathed drinking rooms of America echoed to a higher, sharper note than was their wont. In the neat, inconspicuous white house on the outskirts of Globe, men strutted, ordered a round for the house, and boasted more. Here was man's business—war! There would be uniforms! Guns! Martial music! Women! Wine!

The women listened—even those in the inconspicuous white house—and regarded the males with brighter eyes.

Through the night Frank Luke, who was to call forth

39

the praises of kings and field marshals, watched in wide-eyed wonder from his hotel-room window; beside him the crippled friend who loved him and who, for the first time, could not follow.

In the shining, empty stillness of sunrise they rode on into the hills. Below them lay the town. A few hours before it had been drunk on whisky and enthusiasm. Now—tired, drab as only utilitarian places can be drab—it slept heavily, to awaken shortly under a new goad.

Double production in the mines! War!

Frank Luke accepted the actual declaration of hostilities apathetically enough. He still considered the conflict a thing apart, and was much more intent upon getting on with his hunting.

However, this attitude altered quickly enough when he returned home in the early autumn.

His oldest sister, Eva, a trained nurse, had volunteered her services to the Red Cross. Edwin, his oldest brother, was training for a commission in the field artillery.

During the months Frank and Elder had been in the hills he had forgotten there was a war, and this new state of affairs to which he returned was something less than pleasing.

He, Frank, should have been the first to enlist. Straightway he took steps to correct the situation.

On September 25, 1917, Frank went to Tucson and enlisted as a private in the Signal Corps, requesting immediate assignment to the flying branch. He was ordered to active duty at the School of Military Aeronautics, Austin, Texas.

With Frank to Tucson had gone Bill Elder. Luke was accepted eagerly, but Bill—

"Sorry," the recruiting officers told him, not unkindly, and the two departed. Not until they reached the street did either speak.

"Wish I could have gone," said Bill, and something in his tone brought the big blond's arm up and across his shoulders.

Frank thought of a dusty, sun-drenched road and two barefoot kids eying each other. He thought of a swirling, tumbling river and a bobbing many-branched mesquite stump. He thought of days and nights in lost mountain pockets of Arizona, and, somehow, it all was inextricably entwined with Bill Elder. He sure would miss old Bill!

"I know how it is," he said consolingly. "But don't you care, Bill. We'll show 'em what Arizona can do!"

We?

Why not? Many a man has backed up against the last wall muttering, "We'll whip 'em! We'll whip 'em!" with nothing but a ragtag of a soul to hear him, and *has* whipped 'em! Perhaps Frank Luke needed something Bill Elder had and was availing himself of it with that "we." Whatever it was, it worked.

Frank Luke *did* show 'em what Arizona could do!

After a speedy return trip to Phoenix and hasty farewells, Frank reported at the Texas ground school. He began his record-making early.

One of the requirements of the ground course was to assemble blindfolded a dismantled machine gun. Luke slapped his machine gun into complete working order in a minute flat—quicker than his nearest competitor.

An instructor, astounded by the Arizonian's speed and accuracy, asked Luke how he had achieved this celerity.

"A gun's a gun," Frank explained, "and when you've handled them as much as I have you get to know something about them."

Although his class had commenced its studies some time before he arrived, Frank made such rapid progress that he was graduated with the others November 23, 1917, and ordered to Rockwell Field, San Diego, California.

He took time out for a brief visit to Phoenix, during which he participated in one last swift, sweet jam with Johnny Akers.

John Akers, later circulation manager of the *Arizona Gazette* in Phoenix, was no spare tire in a mix-up. But Johnny didn't want any part in this one and attempted to dissaude Frank from entering it.

Returning from a party late one night, they had taken a short cut through the outskirts of the Mexican quarter, and one of a group of six Mexicans made a slighting remark Luke did not like. He turned and spat Spanish at them.

Akers, realizing little was to be gained in a fight with the odds at six to two, cautioned Frank in a low tone and, when he saw the Mexicans moving toward them, turned quickly.

"Run!" he urged.

"Run, hell!" Luke replied, and squared around to the shuffling Mexicans.

"But they'll knife us!" pleaded Akers, well schooled in Mexican fighting tactics.

"If one of 'em does I'll jam his knife down his throat," said Frank, and shot a punch at the nearest one of the group. That started it.

When Akers described the battle to me, he paused at this point in his story and grinned reminiscently.

"What happened next?" I asked.

"I took a ten-pound sock on the nose," he continued; "then I backed up to Frank and went to work."

"How did you come out?"

"With the scruff of my neck in Frank's hand. He dragged me out after he had kicked those Mexicans round. I wish I hadn't been too busy to watch it, because it must have been a beautiful scrap."

A day or two later Frank went on to California to continue his flying studies and Akers enlisted in a heavy artillery unit soon to see active service in France.

One of his first acts upon arriving at the San Diego flying field was to write his younger brothers John and Bill. These letters, treasured possessions of the two boys when they had grown to young manhood, follow.

DEAR JOHN:

Have not as yet received a letter from you. What's the matter, have you forgotten me? How would you like to take a ride in an airplane? Well, if you are a good boy and study real hard I will take you for a long ride some day. It has auto riding skinned all to pieces. Lots of fun.

Are you being a good boy and helping mother as you should? I hope so. I will have to close, for I still must write a line or two to Bill.

Your brother,
FRANK.

Bill's letter reads:

Bill, the youngest Luke, in a way picked up the workaday things where Frank put them aside. He grew to be tall, muscular, bronzed, and uncommonly like Frank.

He used Frank's favorite gun, that twenty-gauge shotgun that once shredded a Senior pennant. One night, years later, Bill introduced me to the weapon. When I returned it to him he held it, stroking the twin barrels reverently.

"It's the best gun in the world," he said.

I believe I will have gone a long way on the road to whatever goal we march toward if, some day, the touch of any possession of mine brings to a young man's eyes the look of deep earnestness I found in Bill Luke's as he held that shotgun.

Not long after Frank wrote his brothers, he sent one to his sister Anna, apologizing for his inability to repay a small loan.

Frank, ever punctilious about money matters, resented the government's involved pay system, which, in the early days of the war, occasioned more than one junior officer many embarrassing moments. He even spoke of resigning, but it is doubtful if even no pay at all could have dulled his zest for flying. The letter to his sister reads:

December 10, 1917.

43

expected and I haven't enough money to buy stationery, let alone pay any of my bills. It sure makes me sore, but I am sure I will be paid in full next month. If I'm not I will be tempted to resign.

You don't know how rotten it makes a fellow feel to realize that he hasn't a cent and will have to stay on the island week after week without even enough money to pay for his laundry.

And Christmas is coming.

I have been getting along fine with my flying. It is real sport and I only hope I hurry through this school and the next. I am to be given one of the fighting machines across the pond, instead of a reconnaissance plane. I will make myself known or go where most of them do.

The weather is ideal for flying and I am glad I was sent to this school rather than to one in the North.

Do you remember those pictures I left with you saying that I would write for them later? Those of Dixie, etc.? Please send them, and my bathing suit also. If you have a picture of mother and father, please send it.

If it wasn't for the Y.M.C.A. here I would not know what to do. They have desks for writing and furnish paper and envelopes. There always is a number of daily papers on the rack and all sorts of magazines and books. It sure is nice.

I will close hoping to hear from you all soon.

Your brother,
FRANK.

Two days after Frank wrote this letter he was permitted to take his first solo flight. He had been warned repeatedly to make this a matter of straight flying, but Frank had other plans. He executed an easy, perfect take-off, slid up to the altitude he desired, then kicked his ship into a loop.

He leveled off, fell into a steep falling leaf—a little too steep, righted her again, then turned her nose down and over.

Below, on the drome, angry and alarmed instructing pilots followed his movements with anxious eyes and cursed him feelingly. They trotted out to meet him as he taxied in.

"You hemstitched idiot!" one bellowed. "Who th' hell told you you could stunt?"

"Nobody," Luke grinned. "I watched a fellow do it this morning and sort of got the knack of it."

They put him on the ground three days for that. But he was too good a flier to be wasted. He wrote his mother in early January and referred to flying as "very common now" —this still only a matter of days since he had first flown alone!

January 7, 1918.

DEAR MOTHER:

I have not heard from you in some time, but hope everyone at home is fine. I am still gaining weight and am in the best of health. I finished the candy and nuts today and they sure were great. I want to thank you again. I also want to thank whoever sent these towels in the separate package. Were they also from you? They sure are beauties.

How was Christmas at home? I suppose great as ever, and what did the kids and you get? I was very sorry to hear that Ed was confined to camp, but I suppose he is out by this time.

Mother, I have met some little girl here. She sure is nice. She and her mother have been taking me to all the parks, beaches, etc. There are some awfully pretty places here. I am invited to take supper with them next Saturday evening and a long drive on Sunday. They treat me very nicely. If things continue like they have been, I will hate to leave here.

I am coming along fine with my flying; it is very common now. Some of the boys who graduated two weeks ago received their commissions yesterday. They have been strutting around here all day. I only wish I could receive my commission before I get my furlough to go home. I don't think there is much chance, because I am asking for my leave as soon as I finish here and it generally takes several weeks before we get our commissions. I suppose you are tired reading this long letter, so I will close.

Love to all,
FRANK.

The little girl Frank hated to leave was Miss Marie Rapson of No. 767 Twelfth Street, San Diego, to whom he became engaged before he left Rockwell Field. Miss Rapson married several years later, and continued to live in San Diego.

Despite the excitement of training for air battles in France and his new love affair, Frank had not forgotten Bill Elder. On January 15 he wrote:

DEAR BILL:

Just a few lines because I have so much to do Saturday and Sunday evenings (the only days we get off) that I nearly forget to go to bed.

I will be through with this course in a few days and am going to get a two-week furlough to go home, so be sure and find some good hunting grounds and we will have a good hunt before I look for Germans.

Today a number of cadets received their commmissions. Gee, I wish I would get mine before I go home! I don't think there is much chance, though. Some of the fellows have had hard luck. Their papers were lost, causing them to wait two or three months for their commissions. Things are getting straightened out so I don't think there will be much trouble from now on.

My service record was lost, so I have not been paid since I've been in the service. But I am going to be paid in full in a few days. I'll have to celebrate.

I'll ring off, for the bull is running low and I've got to write Pinney a letter.

Your pal,
FRANK LUKE, JR.

On January 23, 1918, Frank was commissioned a second lieutenant in the Aviation Section, Signal Officers Reserve Corps, and given the customary two-weeks' leave before reporting at a port of embarkation for transportation overseas.

He returned immediately to Phoenix, but that last good hunt he had planned with Bill Elder was never taken. Frank was too busy. There was equipment to buy, farewells to be said, parties to be attended.

The day Frank was to leave for the East and France he sought out Bill Elder. Like desert dusk, the war had surrounded him imperceptibly and now it demanded its first sacrifice—separation from Bill Elder.

46

Tears, unashamed tears, stood in Elder's eyes as he gripped Luke's hand.

"Please, Frank," he begged, "can't you make them let me go with you?"

To Bill Elder it was a natural request: Frank Luke could make anyone do anything.

Frank held the steadfast little man's hand tighter. Here was a precious thing, this friendship. He would not find its like again in life.

When he spoke he spoke seriously, for he was making a promise.

"Stick it out, kid," he counseled. "I'll be a major soon and then I'll make 'em send you as my orderly."

Frank Luke meant that, and Bill Elder, sensing it, was content. Frank wanted him.

They never saw each other again.

V

IN March, 1918, the Allied colors drooped perilously near the dust. Driven by the lacerating bayonets of von Bülow's and von Böhm's picked shock troops, sundered and disorganized by the massed artillery of von der Marwitz's and von Hutier's commands, Gough's Fifth British Army was forced into a blind, stumbling, thirty-mile rout.

Along their own sectors the French were retiring, but it was a slower, more stubbornly contested retreat. The mud that caked their boots was French mud. Each shattered town they grudgingly yielded to the gray horde was a French town. The Hun might push them back until they drowned in the English Channel, he might dictate his vaunted Paris peace, but, by the living God, the price of it would be all that even a victor could pay!

Fresh American troops brigaded with the French and British played a bigger part in stemming that last great German offensive than they ever have been, or ever will be, credited with.

We still were looked upon skeptically, and if, during the days the beaten armies shuffled slowly back toward Paris, anyone had said that a twenty-year-old second lieutenant, then en route to France, would be of more value than an army corps in the Allied victories to come, that person would have been regarded as insane.

Probably the only man in the world who would have believed such a seemingly absurd statement was Frank Luke, the recently commissioned pilot who was to astound the fighting world.

I have said that Luke had promised himself greatness. He had. The urge to stand above the ruck of common men made him a remarkable athlete, helped him whip bigger and stronger men. It never left him, and his entire psychology finds terse summation in that line in a letter to his sister:

"I will make myself known or go where most of them do."

Leadership, recognition, a place among his fellows, and a high place visible to all—these were the gifts Frank Luke craved. It is peculiarly fitting that they came to him through the medium of war.

Luke the clerk, the student in a profession, the young business executive, could not have held our attention. But Lieutenant Frank Luke, Jr., the sky rider, the dragoon who charged from out the clouds at dusk, the Balloon Buster of Arizona—as such he is a figure for the ages. There is carven marble, the unfading ink of history, legend, and song, for such as he.

How much of this concerned Luke when he sailed out of New York harbor March 4, 1918, never will be known. None of it, probably. It is doubtful if he even knew that the Allies, whose cause he was to help so vastly, were woefully near the heart-breaking end of things.

He did know that he was headed for France to fly a plane and kill Germans. Why? Well, duty, for one thing. What is duty? You tell me and I'll rebuild you a better world. The Allies hated the Germans—he had been told that—but what had hate to do with him?

In spirit Frank Luke was a boy, a courageous stripling; and hate, like jealousy, is for old men and weaklings.

Nothing in his letters, his conversations with brother officers, or in his personal bearing gives us the right to believe that he regarded himself as a Savior of Democracy, a Crusader for Christ and Humanity.

Like countless others who paid their way with smashed bodies and blood, he was willing to let the Four-Minute speakers and the high-pressure Liberty Bond salesmen consider themselves thus sacredly.

With him, participation in the war was a duty, and he wrote of it as such during the sea interlude before he traveled the glory and the gory road that led to a grave behind a shell-wrecked house of God in Murvaux.

In a letter to his father, written on March 3, 1918, the day before he sailed, he said:

DEAR DAD:

I am now aboard the old German Vaterland, one of the largest and most up-to-date ships afloat. It sure is some boat, just like a large hotel, and as comfortable as one.

The name has been changed to the Leviathan.

I am feeling great but I suppose I will be seasick for, you know, I never have been on the water before. This is the worst time of the year to cross, for it is very rough.

Of course these large boats are not so rough as the smaller ones.

All of the boys are feeling fine and I know we are going to have a good trip.

Now, if anything happens to me, I don't want you to feel bad, for you know I have done my duty and enjoy doing it.

Even if it comes to the worst, my insurance is paid up to date, $10,000 with the government and $1,000 with the Equitable Life. I know that nothing is going to happen but I am telling you just the same.

I spent that hundred dollars you sent me in equipping myself.

I did not write and tell mother of my going until the last thing, for I will be across before she will have time to worry.

Everything is fine and I am in the best of health. I have plenty of extra money that may be needed on the other side. I will not be able to write you for fifteen or twenty days.

Give my best regards to all.

Your son,
FRANK.

Read this letter again, for therein you will find much to prove that Frank Luke, the grinning young hellion, the easy-going buckaroo, was fine, splendid, kindly, considerate. I have said he was arrogant. Let me say here that he could be compassionate too.

"I did not write and tell mother of my going until the last thing."

We all know men who would have done the opposite because their stature as a hero about to enter martyrdom would have been enhanced. There was too much of the real man in Luke for that. He knew that his mother had other children, other worries. Why add to her burden with a detailed chronicle of his dangerous adventures far afield?

That "all of the boys are feeling fine and I know we are going to have a good trip" is Youth thumbing its nose at the world. Maybe there was a war some place, but who gave a damn?

On the other hand, there is stark, naked realism, a kind of grim bargaining with death, in the reference to his insurance. He tells his father not to worry if he falls under the bludgeon of war, and couples the thought with insurance, money, recompense.

Recompense!

What blind, self-centered ass first conceived the idea that dead lips, once able to talk, to smile, to kiss, could be compensated for with gold? It savors of a king's gesture, and a craven king's; so chalk it down to some scented monarch who bought his battles, his women, and his throne with the lives and loves and honor of other men!

But young Luke's association of a death that might await him behind some far horizon and a sum of money is, in itself, an indication of character. Vaguely he realized that there is a debt owed by son to father, and this insurance was one arrangement he had made to meet the obligation.

Frank Luke did not fear death; he did dread its ignominious aftermath. To have girls who had smiled upon him forget his charms, to have men who disliked him cloak their rancor with mock sorrow and mumble commonplace praises—these lacked the color and the dignity of the living great.

He needn't have worried. Long years after men who outlived him to pile minor achievement upon mediocre conquest are dead and forgotten, fathers still will tell their boys the story of Frank Luke with its inevitable closing line:

"There, my son, was a man!"

Luke's family learned first of his arrival in France through a short note to his mother, which follows:

March 19, 1918.

DEAR MOTHER:

I am feeling great and enjoying my trip. I am very sorry that I cannot write and tell you all about it, but you know the censors will not allow it. It sure makes it hard to write when we are so restricted, but this card will let you know that I am fine and having a good time.

I am going down to the Chateau de Blois this afternoon. It is very historical, was built in the Fourteenth Century, and has played a great part in French history. I like France. Everything is so old and the buildings are made of stone and most of them have great stone fences about them. Love to all,

FRANK.

A few days later, March 23, he wrote more of his impressions in a letter to his father:

DEAR DAD:

I arrived in Paris o. k. after a wonderful trip. I have seen quite a bit of the country, but it is strange because everything seems so old and out-of-date. The old churches and chateaus are beautiful. All of these old buildings are surrounded by great stone fences. I have seen many historical places connected with Joan of Arc, Napoleon, etc., but, unfortunately, I cannot tell you of them because this would be revealing my station, which is prohibited.

The war certainly has brought great hardships to many, although the food condition is not bad in this country. With our help they are sure of victory. The American soldiers are treated well by the French, whose worst habit is overcharging.

I took four Phoenix boys to dinner the other night. I think they enjoyed it very much. I know I did. While I have been having officers' mess they have been eating enlisted men's food. The boys were S. Halderman and Fuk-way, old Phoenix High football players in '14; Norman Dunbar, who came to Phoenix last year, and Slim Fad-lock from the Phoenix Fire Department, who is a sergeant. They are the first Phoenix boys I have seen since leaving San Diego. They were up at Camp Funston with Ed and played football with him there.

I am in the best of health and really anxious to finish my training so I can match my skill with some of those Hunfliers. I am not at a concentration camp, but will soon be leaving for one. I am certainly anxious to get there as I have not had a machine in my hands for over a month.

Will close with love to all,

FRANK.

On April 3 Frank wrote to Bill Elder, and the opening line of his letter suggests a previous missive since landing in France. Elder later recalled vaguely a short letter from Luke mailed in England, but he could not find it.

If this is so, Bill Elder, Frank's companion in so many escapades and expeditions, was the first for whom he recorded his arrival in the battle land.

In his April 3 letter Luke wrote:

DEAR BILL:

Wrote you some time ago but have not heard from you yet. I suppose it is the long time it takes mail to travel. I have had some trip. On our way over we were supposed to have run into three subs.

The destroyers that were with us crossed the path of one of them and dropped two depth bombs.

We heard them go off, but I haven't run into anyone who really saw the subs. They claim one of them was destroyed, for they saw oil and stuff rise to the surface.

I didn't like England so well for everything seemed so dirty. Kids would run out all over asking for money. It is bad in France, but not so bad as England.

The English farming country is beautiful. Being spring, everything was covered with a pretty coat of moss and there were beautiful hedges everywhere.

France is a very pretty country, everything seems so

old. Great churches and chateaus all surrounded by great stone fences. I have seen many places made famous by Joan of Arc, Napoleon, etc.

I have not started to fly yet as the weather has been holding us up, but I will in a few days. We have classes every day and they are really interesting. I suppose because it is such vital stuff.

Everything must be learned thoroughly now for it will come in handy when I meet some of my Hun enemies.

The morals of France are just about like you have heard of them. About every other place is a wine shop.

Well, boy, sure would like to hear from you. My address is Lieutenant Frank Luke, Jr., Air Service, United States Reserves, A. E. F., France.

Again in this letter Luke dwells on the evidences of age about him. Old churches, old châteaux, and particularly those old stone walls. Sturdy walls, grayed and moss-covered by the centuries, must indeed have seemed strange to this lad accustomed to vast reaches of desert and grazing land fenced only by the horizon.

Not that he never had observed monuments to time. As a boy in his own Arizona, he had ridden to and beyond the ruins at Casa Grande—old, ages old, when Vásquez de Coronado and his gayly caparisoned caballeros discovered them in their search for the fabled Seven Cities of Cibola.

But the dwellers at Casa Grande were dead—dust to be wind-blown about the rampart-like walls that still stand to mark their passing. This French age was different: it was France itself, a France matured by years that came gracefully, touching lightly the landscape and the homes as sometimes it touches mellowing *grandes dames* and old gentlemen. Here the dwellers still lived as though age did not kill them.

And through this setting, which so impressed him, moved the mighty, breath-taking pageant of France and England and his homeland at war.

Luke's first permanent station in these colorful surroundings was the Third Aviation Instruction center at Issoudun. From there he wrote his next letter to Elder:

DEAR PAL:

Received, two days ago, your letter of March 5 and was very glad to hear from you. Pidge and Perry, from what I hear, failed to get in. It seems that at the time they reached Los Angeles the War Department sent orders not to enlist any more for the aviation branch. I would have liked to have seen Pinney get in. He sure would have had to study, no bluff.

I just passed a double-seater motorcycle. One of the fellows was carrying a pilot who had run into a tree and smashed his head. Gee, it was a tough sight! His eyes were bulged out and his head was one mass of blood. He died a short while after reaching the hospital.

The trouble was a bad fog came up just after he left the ground. He tried to land before it reached him but was too late, lost his way, and hit the tree.

Oh, boy, it's great to be up flying, practicing stunts, and looking down on the earth spread out beneath you. But there are always the new graves, in some of them fellows you knew; there because of a faulty machine or bad judgment. Well, boy, it may be me next but don't tell anyone what I have told you. I would hate to have my mother hear of it, because I tell her it is the safest branch of the service.

My address is on the envelope.

Your pal,
FRANK.

What a picture of Frank Luke! A brother pilot dying before his eyes, the new graves of others, the thought of faulty machines and bad judgment—either one of which might one day kill him, concern lest his mother worry, and above it all that note of sheer gutty defiance:

"Oh, boy, it's great to be up flying!"

A week after he wrote this letter to Elder, Frank, like almost every other member of the American Expeditionary Forces, started a diary. He began it with a commonplace reference to his transfer to Field Five and for a time kept a detailed record of his activities at Issoudun.

The first interesting entry is dated April 29. It follows:

Foggy. Attended inspection of machine classes in the morning. Fog cleared. Had about one and a half hours' flying and practiced twelve landings. Landings mostly good. Had one narrow escape. After cutting off power I wanted to catch it again and cut power high, intending to have motor pull me in. Tried but motor would not catch. Saw trees ahead. A long row of them. Could not go around, so kept up my natural glide and zoomed between two of them. The good Lord caused that gap. For that entire line of trees was unbroken at all other points. I had to put my plane at about eighty degrees to get between them.

The excerpts from Luke's diary have been copied from the original with painstaking care. Those terse, curt sentences are so characteristic of him in action; quick, energy-saving, every swing a blow landed. This is even more startlingly apparent in his combat reports.

In his diary he set down a clipped, vivid account of his narrowest escape from death as a student pilot. It appears under the date of May 1:

Went up to make spirals. Came down feeling I had spiraled at ninety degrees. Instructor said it was pretty good and that I had done about sixty degrees. Went up again and think I brought her nearer ninety degrees. My last spiral climbed 3,000 feet. Thought I would make a sideslip, so threw her into it. After a 500-foot drop I started pulling her out. The tail made a swing, nearly throwing me from the machine. My belt came unfastened. I caught the upper wing with my left hand and saved myself. The next minute I was in the bottom of the machine jammed up against the controls.

By the time I recovered my position in the seat I had dropped about 1,000 feet and was going at terrific speed. I tried to sideslip, nose dive, everything to get out, but it was of no use. It seemed useless and I felt that in the next minute I would crash. As luck would have it I came out about 100 feet from the ground, nearly stalled, but dove and made a nice landing. That was so close that it made it very uncomfortable.

In a very short time machines were flying overhead looking for me. They thought I had crashed. Three motorcycles were at hand and I was told that two ambulances were on the way, but I did not see either of them. The first mechanic who arrived on a motorcycle said they had seen me come down from Field Four and that I was coming at such a terrific rate of speed that he became sick. He said that if I had hit at the rate I was traveling they wouldn't have been able to find the tail because it would have been buried. I went up and made another spiral and went home to my field.

When most men have come through an experience such as the one Luke describes, they remain fear-shaken, dazed for hours. How did it affect him?

"I went up and made another spiral."

It is easy to believe that this was the man who, in the words of his Group Commander, Major Harold E. Hartney, "was the nerviest, most courageous pilot who ever took a combat plane off the ground!"

The day after the episode of the broken belt, Luke took his plane to 12,000 feet, the highest he had flown yet. The days that followed brought a series of minor crashes and forced landings, the first on May 3. He wrote:

I started at 7:30 for Dommartin but had a forced landing over the woods. I made for the field but the wind drifted me into a ditch and I turned over. I hurt my shoulder and leg slightly. I smashed the wings, rudder, propeller, and engine hood. French people rushed over to the machine and pulled me out from under the wreck and investigated my arm to see if it was broken. They brought me a bottle of wine. Major Bunnell came by in a new Packard and ran off the road. He told me that a Hun had come down with a broken wing at Dommartin. I had a nice dinner at a French farm and was treated fine that night. A Ford machine came out for the wreck and took it back to Issoudun. I went in a two-seater motorcycle, with Victor Pichard, who was flying a hundred-and-twenty horse-power from Field Eight and he saw me spin in. He came down to see if I needed help and on landing broke his undercarriage. Found a good hotel and stayed the night. Next day I met some very nice girls.

On May 6 he recorded another forced landing:

Read in the morning. In the afternoon took a trip to Dommartin, Worthy Struthers and myself. On landing my motor was missing. I had it fixed and started out again in the rain. My motor went bad but I landed again. I had a broken pusher rod. The others went back and Worthy got lost. I slept at the Angleterre Hotel. The next morning I met two Paris girls.

In an entry marked, "May ninth to the fifteenth," he wrote:

Rained. Have had several tail spins and one sideslip of 1,500 feet.

For May 17 his diary records:

Had a two-hour formation and I was leader. Next formation McCord was leader. I was out of gas. A French-woman asked me if I was married. I told her "no," and she said, "Neither is my girl," pointing to a sixteen-year-old girl. Walked two miles to get gas.

On May 20 he again tasted praise, and from a source that must have pleased him, for it was Quentin Roosevelt who lauded his flying ability. The diary entry reads:

Formation morning. Did stunts. In the afternoon was leader of a world-beater formation. Roosevelt said, "Best formation pulled off at camp." In the afternoon contour flying. Left bunch. Started to pull up for telephone wires. Motor died. Sharp turn to the left. Small field. High grass. Rough. Just pulled over into a vegetable garden. Landed o. k. Hard time getting out. Field so small and grass so high did not leave ground until just about on ditch, then I nearly turned over on the wing.

Two days later he reports another crash:

Had a new ship given to me. No. 445. Started up and at about 500 feet pusher rod broke and tore off hood. Landed in small field o. k. On ground rest of day. Ruined motor. Made two holes in top wing. Noise very loud. Large pieces of tin flew in all directions.

On May 30 Luke, with several other pilots, was ordered to Cazau in southern France for further training. Frank had spent most of the morning playing with several French children who had been befriended by the fliers. One of the aviators urged him to hurry with his packing so they all could take the same train.

Luke turned to the smiling, wistful children who had suspended their play until this so grand American could rejoin them. He grinned a little sheepishly.

"You fellows go ahead," Frank said. "I'll meet you in Cazau. I gotta play with these kids."

VI

RAIN—a cold, wet rain that belied the promise of summer the arrival of June had given—beat sullenly, monotonously on the hangars and squat barracks of the airdrome at Cazau.

The wind sock—bedraggled, forlorn, like one of the drooping ostrich plumes that once appeared in almost every police court after a hilarious and rainy Saturday night—hung soddenly against its pole outside the Operations Office.

Wisps of gray fog, water-slashed, sifted an aimless course low over the widening puddles that blotched the landing field with yellow rash.

From the hangars, propellers occasionally spank-spanked the wet air listlessly, hesitated, missed a blow, ceased, and were still. Grimed mechanics, elbow-deep in the bowels of motors, spoke in monosyllables or allowed irritably voiced questions to pass unanswered.

In the officers' mess, pilots, made doubly nervous by inaction, drank, walked to the windows, cursed the rain, the war, the commanding officer, the rain—walked back to sprawled groups at tables and drank again.

Into this atmosphere of surly resignation Frank Luke entered enthusiastically. With him through the wide-flung door came the even tempo of rain on soggy turf, the protestations of an overburdened truck, and a bugle's flat blat from somewhere summoning someone to do something. The pilots greeted him sourly:

"Close that damn' door!"

"Where the hell d'ye think y'are, Arizona?"

"What have you got to grin about?"

Luke beamed on his disgruntled messmates.

"I've got orders to quit this dump; that's what I've got to grin about," he announced.

"Where you going?"

They gathered about him eagerly, their fed-upness giving way to interest in Luke's orders, for it was from Cazau that men went up to the combat outfits to find fame, bronze for their chests, and acedom—or bleak white crosses beside piles of blackened, twisted salvage metal. Or both.

"Combat work," Luke informed them, although that was slightly more than his orders indicated. "I've been ordered to the acceptance park at Orly."

Many in the group were duly impressed, but an older pilot laughed scornfully.

"Combat, hell!" he snorted. "You'll get more combat work if you stay here and try to make one of the C. O.'s dames. You'll just be a lousy ferryman, that's what you'll be. Just a lousy ferryman."

Luke continued to smile. "Anyway," he said, "it'll be better than this hole."

The others agreed profanely.

"Just a lousy ferryman," precisely describes Frank's position at Orly. It became his duty to fly new planes to combat units nearer the lines and, whenever possible, pilot ships unfit for battle service back to the repair depot. It was about as exciting as being a conductor on a commuters' train.

It did give him opportunities to become intimately acquainted with almost every type of plane flown by the Allies, and materially increased his ability as a pilot.

But the endless monotony of up to the front—back to the base—up to the front—and back to the base again galled Luke. He wanted action, and beefed about it so much that other ferry pilots grew to dislike him.

"What's biting this bird?" they asked. "Think he's any better than we are? He's not the only guy who wants to get off this station, but yowling about it isn't going to help."

Perhaps it did, for on July 26, 1918, Luke received his assignment to a combat unit.

"You lucky stiff!" the other pilots growled enviously and sped him on his way.

Luke joined the First Pursuit Group at Saints in the Aisne-Marne salient. The First Pursuit needed pilots badly. The going had been rough and the casualties heavy, including such men as Raoul Lufbery, Quentin Roosevelt, Malcolm Gunn, James Miller, and Philip Davis.

The remaining pilots had arrived at the stage where it took four drinks to get the kick normally obtained from two. They realized that a man couldn't live forever and that having your skull caved in when the instrument board crushed back on you was part of being a hero, but you couldn't put on much of a dawn patrol with dead men.

The need of the moment was fliers—live ones. They'd pep up the outfit, too, with their bright-eyed eagerness for killings and confirmations and medals.

Dear God, they'd all known that eagerness—once!

The draft of which Luke was a member arrived at troop headquarters in the hushed dark of midnight, the silence broken only by the doleful, hollow thud of their boots as they walked toward the lights in the Adjutant's office.

This was different. They sensed it. There was something tensed, vitally alert about this sleeping drome that had not marked other stations. The playing at soldier stood behind them now. The war itself was here.

This impression was intensified when they entered the Adjutant's office. Although the hour was late, there was considerable activity among a number of officers present, who stood about silently while the newcomers presented their orders.

Nor did the fresh fliers miss the strained look about the eyes, the peculiar nervous repose that marked these new silent brothers-in-arms. The replacement men—shuffling, uncomfortable, in their first contact with the terse, curt manners of an advanced flying field—noted, too, on most of the tunics, a row of varicolored ribbons beneath the silver wings. The ribbons represented medals, the medals were symbolic of some nation's recognition, and a nation's recognition now meant battle, conquest, death!

This was one of the things for which they had come—a ribbon. Bronze for their chests!

Across the room one man stood alone, not quite smiling nor quite austere. His lean body, slack in an easy posture, spelled capability, a lazy grace that might instantly become decisive action, and among the newcomers the whisper spread:

"Rickenbacker!"

They eyed him furtively, for here was one of their gods —here, within reach. Would they ever be as great as he? Would they, too, come to wear a rainbow splash of color under their silver wings?

Before the summer was over, Rickenbacker the mighty was to regard with respectful awe one of these novices. He was to see the ribbon he coveted most—the starred ribbon of the Congressional Medal of Honor—go to one of these abashed youngsters, Frank Luke. The day was nearing when he would say of him:

"Luke was the greatest fighter who ever went into the air!"

But as Luke stood with the others before the Group Adjutant he was just a blond shavetail blinking at the light—and probably homesick. In response to the Adjutant's dismissal, he clumped off in the wake of a sleepy sergeant major to his new quarters.

Luke, with several others, went down to the Twenty-seventh Squadron, then commanded by Major Harold E. Hartney, soon to take over the First Pursuit Group.

That night, and for many nights thereafter, Luke and the others who had come up with him listened to a new, an ominous sound: a surging, restless beat that may well be called the basic minor note of war—the feet of men on roads!

They passed within a short distance of the flying field, an endless column throbbing out the news of its pilgrimage in vagrant, broken discord or in measured, heavy melody.

As a lad Luke had reveled in the paced rhythm of Kipling's "Boots." He could understand that piece of writing now.

Foot—foot—foot—foot—sloggin' over Africa—

No, that wasn't right.

Foot—foot—foot—foot—sloggin' up to Germany—

That was it—Germany! That's where the feet were going!

Feet of men who would not pass that way again. Feet of youths who, like himself, were just realizing that women are soft and sweet and lovable, that wine warms the belly and the heart, and that songs are made to be sung. Feet thumping out their minor chords to the accompanying *Miserere* of the guns that now saturated the air, as the heavy bass notes of an organ perfume an empty church with sound.

Feet!

Thank God, he didn't have to walk to war!

The next day Major Hartney held a formation to address the new pilots.

"If you survive the first two weeks you're well over the hill," he informed them bluntly, and continued: "I'm not trying to discourage any of you, but you may as well know what you're up against. Some of you are certain to be washed out during the first two weeks. If you get through that period safely, you'll probably accomplish things. That's all, gentlemen."

Pleasant, that, to have a determined-looking little runt—Hartney *was* a runt in those days—tell you he expects to have you spin in within fourteen days!

It was at this, their first meeting, that Hartney's attention centered on Luke. Hartney, later head of General Airways, Inc., of New York City, told me that he was conscious of Luke's presence during his entire talk.

"In a way, I resented his attitude," Luke's first combat commander said. "He seemed to be saying: 'Don't kid me. I'm not afraid of the bogy man.' When I had finished talking he was grinning. That ruffled me, too.

64

"But I came to love him and to have downright respect for him before long. Man, how that kid could fly! No one —mind you, no one—had the sheer contemptuous courage that boy possessed. I know he's been criticized for being such a lone-hander, but, good Lord, he won us priceless victories by those very tactics.

"He was an excellent pilot and probably the best flying marksman on the Western Front. We had any number of expert pilots and there was no shortage of good shots, but the perfect combination, like the perfect specimen of anything in the world, was scarce. Frank Luke was that perfect combination."

It must not be forgotten, however, that this is in retrospect. Luke, in the days of his combat apprenticeship in the Twenty-seventh Squadron, was just another pilot detailed there for duty, and a not too popular pilot at that. The Twenty-seventh had some good men on its rolls, and Frank was inclined to talk a little too much for a newcomer who hadn't shown his stuff.

It was all right to say you were good, but these proved fliers—many of them already aces—weren't taking anyone's word for it. They didn't have to.

All were willing to admit that Luke was a competent airplane chauffeur. His record showed that. However, there was a good deal more to the business than the comparatively simple process of taking a plane off the ground, joy riding around a bit, and setting her down again.

There must be fighting sense—staff officers call it air strategy—for one thing; there must be the ability to coordinate gun and rudder, head and hand, for another; and there must be the killing instinct, for a third.

These further degrees of air craftsmanship Luke had not yet displayed. He didn't keep them waiting long.

His first flight over the lines was in a formation led by Major Hartney. The green fliers were securely hedged about by experienced pilots, for there were wolves in the cloud hills and these lambs must be protected.

Although this was Luke's first trip into hostile territory, he seized upon it as the first opportunity to conduct himself in a manner that subsequently not only added to his spectacular fame, but frequently brought down upon him the broiling wrath of his superiors.

He quit the flight to sail off on his own!

Hartney was waiting for him when he came in many minutes after the patrol had returned and the pilots dispersed.

"Where the hell did *you* go?" he barked.

Green pilots who prospected on their own were not popular in any squadron. Their defalcation might cause the annihilation of an entire flight.

"I had engine trouble," Luke explained blandly.

This was entirely possible, so Hartney let it pass. But when, on the second patrol thereafter, Luke again deserted the formation, Hartney advanced upon him fuming.

There was no willingness to accept reprimand in Luke's attitude. He replied truculently:

"I got a Hun!"

"The hell you did! Where?"

Luke couldn't locate precisely where this combat had taken place, with the result that it became the greatest controversial air battle in the American Air Service. Luke was —still is—called a windjammer, a four-flusher, and an out-and-out old-fashioned, four-letter liar because of that victory he claimed to have won over German territory.

Laurence La Tourette Driggs, in his admirable book, *Heroes of Aviation,* attempts to confound the Arizonian with his own combat report, but the weight of evidence is against Mr. Driggs.

In the chapter devoted to Luke, Mr. Driggs quotes one of his combat reports wherein Frank says, "This was my first combat," as proof positive that Luke's claim was spurious.

But Mr. Driggs erroneously dates the report September 16 instead of August 16. The latter date is the one the original—which I have seen—bears, and it is Luke's first combat report. Unquestionably, this account, which follows in full, is the one he rendered:

Combat Report—August 16, 1918.

Lieutenant Frank Luke reports:

My machine was not ready, so left an hour after formation expecting to pick them up on the lines, but could not find formation. Saw Hun formation and followed, getting above, into the sun. The formation was strung out leaving one machine way in the rear. Being way above the formation, I cut my motor and dove down on the rear man, keeping the sun directly behind. Opened fire at about 100 feet, keeping both guns on him until within a few feet, then zoomed away. When I next saw him he was on his back, but looked as though he was going to come out of it, so I dove again, holding both guns on him. Instead of coming out of it he sideslipped off the opposite side, much like a falling leaf, and went down on his back.

My last dive carried me out of reach of another machine that had turned about. They gave chase for about five minutes, then turned back, for I was leading them. My last look at the plane shot down convinced me that he struck the ground, for he was still on his back about 1,500 meters below.

On coming home above our lines saw four E. A. [enemy aircraft]. Started to get into the sun and above, but they saw me and dove towards me. I peaked for home.

Three turned back and the other came on. I kept out of range by peaking slightly and he followed nearly to Coincy, where he saw one of the Ninety-fifth [Squadron] boys and turned about. The Ninety-fifth man could have brought down this E. A. if he had realized quick enough that it was an E. A.

The machine [the first he refers to] was brought down northeast of Soissons in the vicinity of Jouy and Vailly. Do not know the exact location as, this being my first combat, did not notice closely, but know that it was some distance within German territory, for Archies [anti-aircraft] followed me for about ten minutes on my way back.

My motor was fixed at Coincy and filled with gas and oil. Also found out that our formation had been held up by the Salmson that it was to escort and had just started. Left the ground to find them. Flew at about 5,000 meters from Soissons past Fismes, but did not see the formation. Saw one Salmson but no E. A. Returned home.

Major Hartney accepted this report and Luke was credited officially with the plane, for it was the first on the list with which the War Department provided me.

Hartney, in discussing this phase of Luke's career, said:

"I am firmly convinced the boy got the plane. His verbal account of the battle contained those little differences that give such a report the touch of verisimilitude. But the squadron didn't believe him and that made Luke bitter."

Bitter it did make him.

Because of this incident, the hot, hard words that bring up the cold, hard fists frequently filled the officers' mess-room at Twenty-seven Squadron. As a result, Luke regarded his brother officers contemptuously, taunted them with their own shortcomings, dared them to fight, and, when they declined, avoided them.

All but one—Joe Wehner.

Lieutenant Joseph Wehner was bitter, too. Wehner, a Bostonian, enlisted in the flying corps at Kelly Field, Texas. Immediately some lumber-skulled intelligence officer saw a menace to the entire Allied military structure in Wehner's presence. Wasn't Wehner a German name? Hadn't he, ostensibly a poor man's son, come all the way from Boston at his own expense to enlist?

But the intelligence officers would thwart this ruthless agent of the Kaiser's spy system!

They did. They followed his every move, and misconstrued them all. They counted the spoonfuls of sugar he used in his coffee and read therein a secret code. They examined his letters and baggage.

Wehner, in protesting this surveillance, spoke freely and heatedly of the childish tactics of certain grown men, the emptiness of certain swelled heads, and the general inconvenience of being persecuted by misguided individuals who were frightened by phantoms their overzealous minds had created.

"Ah, ha!" said the misguided ones. "He is becoming desperate!"

Whereupon they slapped Wehner into close arrest.

When the Twenty-seventh Squadron left Texas, Wehner was still under arrest. Cleared of any taint of treasonable conduct, he sped to New York to join his squadron, and was arrested by Secret Service agents.

Permitted to sail with his unit, further indignity awaited

him when he landed in France. A third time he was shadowed, detained, questioned, frowned upon, and dismissed with the warning that his every move would be followed.

What imbecility! If he was a spy he should have been backed up against a wall and shot. Found innocent, he should have received an apology and no further molestation. Follow his every move? I doubt it. It took honest courage to go where Joe Wehner went, and you can't "frame" that.

What did all this do to Wehner? First, it made him an outcast in his own mind. He suspected the man who sat beside him at mess. He doubted the genuineness of the snores that rumbled from the cot adjoining his. Then it made him a hellcat in action; a looping, soaring, shooting fool who drove a bullet-riddled plane as a pursued rider drives a tired horse—mercilessly.

When the squadron sneered its disbelief of Luke, Wehner went to him. Here was another injustice, and it forged a bond between them.

They became the deadliest duo that ever soared aloft. Bishop? Nungesser? Rickenbacker? Richthofen? Squadron men, all. These madmen just out of their teens were lonehanders. With Wehner riding the sun and Luke to do the strafing, they brought new flame to the twilight skies of the Western Front, undying honor to their service, and demoralization to German balloon observation.

Joe Wehner plunged to his death protecting Luke. Frank went to his, avenging Joe Wehner.

Luke and Wehner—liar and spy?

If you could shout their names to the four far walls of Valhalla, the scarred battle dead of the ages would roar you the reply:

"Luke? Wehner? Aye, we know them!"

VII

THE controversy over Luke's first victory was still the principal topic of conversation in the Twenty-seventh Aëro Squadron when Major Hartney left that unit to take over the First Pursuit Group, of which the Twenty-seventh was a part.

Captain Alfred A. Grant, afterwards a successful Los Angeles businessman, succeeded to the command. Grant did not believe Luke's story, nor was he ever personally attracted to the Arizonian. Although they were reared in similar schools—Grant is a Texan—it is doubtful if you could find two more widely opposed personalities than Alfred Grant and Frank Luke.

Both possessed great courage—among his decorations Captain Grant has the Distinguished Service Cross for intrepidity in air combat; both were leaders by instinct, but they were separated by a vast difference in mental attitude.

Captain Grant was an orderly soldier, who believed regulations were written for a purpose. He was a disciplinarian.

Frank Luke chafed at discipline, fretted under regimentation, and bridled at authority.

"Too happy-go-lucky to know his own talents," one of the Phoenix High School yearbooks said of him, and his army superiors will add: "Too damned independent to do anything he didn't want to do."

It was a natural independence, born and fostered in his

homeland, the open, rugged Southwest. No man can stand on his own from the boyhood years, as Frank Luke did, and not place a high valuation on his own abilities, and a still higher valuation on his freedom of action. Jam such a man into a mold, any mold, and you have a rebel.

Luke's rebellion was not founded on independence alone. The old urge to do things still motivated him, and there had been added—bitterness.

How many of the mighty accomplishments of all time are owed to some sorehead who did it "to show them"?

Frank was bitter. He was, so far as the picayune details of army life were concerned, in rebellion. But let this be remembered: he never questioned a combat order, he never groused at discomfort, nor whined under hardship. Hardship, discomfort, danger—these were dishes he relished and of which he was to have his fill in the few short weeks of life remaining to him.

During this period the massed assault that was to leave 150 square miles of German-occupied territory in the St. Mihiel sector in American hands was taking shape. This tremendous military maneuver, part of the colossal movement of armies which began the German rout ending in the Armistice on November 11, brought Frank his fame, his high place, the bronze for his chest . . . bronze he never wore; medals he did not know he had won.

As part of the battle plan, the First Pursuit Group returned to the Verdun sector and established its headquarters at Rembercourt, a dozen miles south of the line. From there Luke continued his desertion of formations, his solo flying.

"Joy riding again," his flight commanders complained wrathfully, and read him the riot act. They might as well have written letters to the *Times;* they'd have accomplished as much.

Luke's favorite misbehavior was to take off from his own field, quit the flight, cruise about on his own; then, instead of returning to his unit, land on the drome of the French Cigognes several miles from the Twenty-seventh's headquarters.

The Cigognes—so called because of the escadrille emblem, a stork, painted on their planes—were exclusive and proud of it. They were a sort of flying Texas Rangers, a band of superheroes, worshiped by the entire French nation, respected by their allies, feared by their enemies.

Officially known as N. 3 because of the Nieuport planes they flew, the Cigognes had gathered fame through the membership of such men as Captain Brocard, the squadron's founder; "Père" Dorme, still a mystery man, for he flew off one day never to return, and no one marked his fall; Captain Heurteaux, who, like the German air giant, von Richthofen, first learned the scientific killing of his fellow men as a cavalry officer; René Fonck, Armand Pinsard, and the incomparable Guynemer.

The very hangars in which the planes of these men rested between combats attracted Luke. Here they moved, laughed, jested. Here they drew in the smoke from a final cigarette before climbing the skies.

The Cigognes regarded Luke and his erratic visits, first with tolerant good humor, then with genuine interest. Droll, this fellow, with his perennial grin and his boy's face, but, you perceived, a face of character. Irresponsible? Of a certainty. As irresponsible as a Montparnasse artist. But what mattered irresponsibility so long as one had courage?

And courage he had. That last take-off, for instance. Only inches between his landing gear and the trees rimming the field. He would die, of course. These precious ones did.

The cursed war! There would be none but old men left, and who would set young breasts to fluttering then?

When, within a few weeks after he first visited them, Frank Luke began to achieve a balloon record surpassing that of any other aviator, the Cigognes looked upon him with amazement.

Whenever he taxied into their field, they ran out to his ship, chattering volubly. They clapped him on the back, crowded about him during the short walk to the mess for a glass of wine, toasted him with exaggerated French courtesy—which is not exaggerated in the French—and were proud of his friendship.

Laugh at Frank Luke because all this brought a ruddy glow of pleasure to his cheeks, a fever glitter to his eyes, stretched his blouse tighter across his chest? Frank Luke had earned it, for even the Cigognes regarded a voluntary attack on an enemy balloon as heroic madness. If one were ordered to strafe a balloon—well, one strafed it. One did as one was ordered in the Cigognes. But to cruise the clouds seeking them? No! Life was precious and one did not toss it away.

There are many excellent reasons for this attitude which may not be entirely clear to the inexperienced.

Because they were anchored to trucks, balloons were much better targets for an aërial gunner than airplanes. Their buoyant cargo of inflammable gas was almost certain to explode when the bag was struck by an incendiary bullet, and even a few well-placed rounds of service ammunition would make the balloon collapse.

Not infrequently the falling sausage killed the observers —from one to four or five highly trained officers—as well as many of the winch and truck crews on the ground. This means casualties, and casualties are an objective of war.

The loss of life coincident to the destruction of a balloon was, however, the least important consideration.

The balloon was one of the most valuable adjuncts to modern artillery. As an observation medium for minor-caliber batteries, most artillerymen considered it superior to the airplane because, while sacrificing little in mobility, it was possible to maintain constant direct telephone communication between observation point and battery.

Every balloon put out of action meant a valuable field of observation closed to operation. This meant erratic battery fire, sometimes none at all; which, in turn, resulted in ragged, inefficient barrages, indecisive support for offensives, and weakened defensive counter-battery fire. Also, balloons, like most of the machinery of war, were expensive, the average one with its equipment costing about $100,000.

These considerations, and the knowledge that a balloon shot down was regarded as an important conquest, caused armies to go to great lengths in protecting the sausages.

Their locations were carefully chosen to facilitate the placing of antiaircraft (Archie) batteries in the immediate vicinity. These batteries—during the World War mostly 75s on special mounts—were augmented by innumerable long-range machine guns and small bomb-throwing cannon. The balloon's fixed position enabled the gunners to range the air about the giant bags with meticulous accuracy.

In addition to these elaborate defenses, there usually was to be found at least a four- or five-ship flight of combat planes sufficiently near balloon-operating points to take the air above the bags immediately after an enemy plane had been sighted.

The pilot who would distinguish himself by strafing balloons must descend into this inferno of shrapnel, machine-gun bullets, and "flaming onions," either pursued by the balloon's protecting planes or with the almost certain knowledge that they would be upon him before he could register on the bag and gain sufficient altitude to fight or or peak for home.

No chivalrous combats of the fathomless blue to be likened to the knight-errantry of old, these balloon rows. Rather should they be compared to the rough-and-tumble maulings of longshoremen's speak-easies. Fights wherein the side with the advantage always won and where both sides used every advantage, fair and foul.

A sudden swoop from the clouds—the shot from behind—was fair; so was the unexpected impact of three-inch high explosive—the knee in the groin. They were brutal, bloody, vicious—these split-second combats a few hundred feet above the earth—but they were vital episodes of modern battle.

This was the field of activity Frank Luke selected as offering the shortest route to military glory, one which would also thoroughly and forever confound those who had doubted him. Nor did he become the world's deadliest balloon buster by accident. He planned it as deliberately as he had planned hunting trips with Bill Elder into the mountains of Arizona.

At the evening meal, September 11, 1918, the talk in the Twenty-seventh Squadron officers' mess blew lightly this way and that, as mess-room chatter will: the fit of this man's pants, the cut of that man's blouse; the latest on the war—authentic, since it came that day from a side-car driver who had a captain who knew an aide who drank with a general

74

who said he saw; the comparative honesty of French *femmes de nuit* and American ladies of the evening; the mishaps of the day.

Luke gave little attention until the talk turned to balloons, and Captain Jerry C. Vasconcelles, an ace and one of the most daring fliers in the Twenty-seventh, said emphatically:

"I think they're the toughest proposition a pilot has to meet. Any man who gets a balloon has my respect, because he's got to be good or he doesn't get it!"

The others nodded solemnly, little realizing that Vasconcelles' words would be indirectly responsible for one of the most amazing individual careers in our military history.

On the following day, while Luke and Wehner stood chatting a few minutes before the flight took off, Luke asked:

"Did you hear what Vasconcelles said about balloons last night?"

"Yes," Wehner replied. "Why?"

"Oh, nothing much," Luke went on, "only I'm going to get one today."

Mechanics who overheard the conversation smiled, and with a tolerant chuckle passed the word:

"Luke's gonna get a sausage. So he says."

And the grinning rejoinder:

"Yeah? So'll the Y. M. C. A. He'll get a mess-kit full of tough language from ol' man Grant if he don't quit cruisin' around France in that Spad of his!"

But there was no tough language for him that day.

In less than two hours after he made the statement that evoked the mechanics' tolerant banter, Luke had crushed his first balloon, single-handed!

It happened over Marieulles, a bruised clutter that had been a town, bored with strife until it became aware of this fly-and-dragon contest above it. And the fly was victorious!

At Lavignéville Luke sighted three enemy aircraft and gave chase, lifting his ship into a faster gait as he once shook out his reins in the pursuit of scurrying jack rabbits. The enemy planes sped east over Pont-à-Mousson and disappeared toward Metz.

He pulled over in the direction of Marieulles, and there,

low above the battered town, bobbing and weaving in the light breeze, rode a balloon!

Up, up he went, because he wanted altitude to drop from. He wanted distance from the earth to fall through, that he might come down at skin-burning speed and strike.

He climbed until the bag was just a speck below him. To his right a soft black smudge spread on the air, soft and fluffy like a splatter of chocolate cream. Soft? Yes, if steel death is soft. That was antiaircraft. The balloon batteries had seen him.

He gave his ship full throttle and dived. Earth and sky lost their accustomed stability and rushed madly at each other. Wind! Wind such as he did not know could be tore at his plane, pulled savagely at wing and strut and stay wire.

Sound! A hellish shrieking as though all the demons ever spawned writhed unseen about him, screaming a protest that penetrated his leather helmet.

Speed! The steady march of his air-speed indicator like a skinny black soldier on parade—125-130 miles an hour. More—135—140—145—150—like a child, its face in its hands standing against a tree counting: "One fifty—155—160—ready or not, I'm coming!"

Ready or not, he *was* coming!

Dozens of black cream puffs around him now. Scores of them. Sky showing where, a moment before, there had been an expanse of gray canvas. The cream puffs did that.

Now! His sight clogged with the balloon's bulk. A squirming, terror-driven thing—a man—fouled in the rigging of the basket! Now! His guns coughed, choked on the vile-smelling phosphorous bullets in their throats, and spat red streams of them at the plump body of the balloon. It jumped under their impact like a fat man who had been prodded in the stomach.

A roaring spiral, a loop, and another burst into the balloon's sagging side. There was no Archie now, the ground batteries holding their fire because of the danger of hitting the balloon and the observers, one of them sinking earthward under a white splash of parachute.

Frantic winch crews applied themselves in a vain attempt to bring the balloon to the ground. Luke's machine guns aided them. They jammed.

76

He swung off to one side, pulled and pushed and slapped the firing mechanism of one gun into working order, and swooped back to the attack.

The balloon was almost on the ground; but he followed, banked in over the leaking bag, and raked it stem to stern with an unbroken sputter of fire from his left gun.

"Who-o-o-o-m!"

A puff of hot, gaseous air kicked him upward. Thick black smoke rolled aloft to obscure and confuse him as he climbed for clear air.

He couldn't get balloons, huh? The hell he couldn't! And they'd want confirmation, would they? All right, they'd get 'em!

He swung back toward the American lines, where he had seen one of his own balloons on his way out, located it, decided to chance a landing in a near-by field, and slanted earthward, contributing a moment of stuttering panic to the observers until they recognized the markings on his ship.

Several of the balloon crew trotted toward him as he bumped in over the uneven field.

"Did you see that Heinie balloon?" he called above the diminishing thump of his propeller.

An observer laughed:

"Did we see it? You're damn tootin' we saw it. There wasn't anything else to see just about then."

Luke chuckled.

"Gimme a confirmation, will you?"

Frank Luke, Jr., became the Balloon Buster of Arizona right there! Armed with two confirmations from witnesses to his exploit, he attempted to fly back to his drome. But he had scarcely taken off when his motor went out on him and he had to return to the balloon field, where he learned his shrapnel-splashed motor could not immediately be repaired.

Frank's first balloon victory had its pathetic side. The squirming, terror-driven little man fouled in the basket rigging was Lieutenant Willy Klemm, a jovial, ruddy-cheeked Bavarian. His commission was new, so new it squeaked, and he was tremendously proud of it.

In the days before the war, Willy Klemm regarded His

Imperial Majesty's officers with awe. Now he was one of them, taking his first flight as a man of importance. It was short-lived. One of Frank's bullets went in under Willy's heart. They freed him from the rigging when the balloon hit the ground, but he died a few days later.

After making arrangements to have his plane transported to the home field, Luke returned in a side car and proceeded immediately to file his combat report.

Read it:

COMBAT REPORT—*September 12, 1918.*
Lieutenant Frank Luke reports:

Saw three E. A. [enemy aircraft] near Lavignèville and gave chase, following them directly east towards Pont-à-Mousson where they disappeared towards Metz. Saw enemy balloon at Marieulles. Destroyed it after three passes at it. Each within a few yards of the balloon. The third pass was made when the balloon was very near the ground.

Both guns stopped, so pulled off to one side. Fixed left gun and turned about to make one final effort to burn it. The next instant it burst into great flames and dropped on the winch, destroying it.

There was a good field near our balloons, so landed for confirmation. The observer, Joseph M. Fox, who saw the burning, said he thought several were killed when it burst into flames so near the ground. Left field and started back when my motor began cutting out. Returned to same field and there found out my motor could not be fixed, so returned by motor cycle. Attached you will find confirmation from Lieutenant Fox and Lieutenant Smith. Both saw burning.

"Attached you will find confirmation"! The insulting guts of the lad risking a crash in a pasture lot not five minutes after a spectacular victory to take a confirmation with him! Here was one victory he would not be talked out of.

The squadron had heard of his feat by telephone from the balloon company and was out to congratulate him when he rolled in. They shook his hand, slapped him on the back, and trooped along with him to his quarters. His ground crew took on new importance and averred trucu-

78

lently that they had known all afternoon he would get a balloon. Hadn't he said so?

The next morning his plane was flown back to the home field to be received by awed mechanics. They had seen other planes come in after combats; they had listened to Luke's own account of his exploit; they knew he had weathered the balloon defenses for three hawklike rushes—still, the condition of the machine awed them.

It was riddled! Riddled, gouged, and splintered where shrapnel and machine-gun bullets had registered on it. The wings were slashed and torn, the fuselage a thing of unsightly punctures. Here a neat, round hole; there a long, jagged gouge. There was a hole through the seat, a shrapnel gash not six inches from his body.

Luke poked his fingers through them and laughed, but his chief mechanic saw nothing humorous in the situation.

"Lieutenant, I've seen a lot of planes come in," he said. "But when they come in this way, the bird that drives 'em gets it and he gets it fast."

Luke grinned at him.

"They can't get me," he replied confidently. "Look at that!"—inserting a finger in the hole through the seat. "Why didn't that one hit me?"

While he lived that was his attitude: "They can't get me!" Warned that his scorn of even the few rules of caution of which a flier may avail himself would kill him, Luke would laugh and ask:

"What's the matter? Afraid?"

The controversy over his first claim of victory still rankled.

Luke had another characteristic, one that has taken a long toll of life—curiosity.

This is best illustrated by a story I have been told by several officers who flew with him. Late one afternoon, when Luke's flight was returning from a patrol, he deliberately swung out of the formation and turned back over the lines. He landed a few minutes after the others had come in. "What, in God's name, did you turn back for?" they demanded.

The quiet sincerity of his answer convinced them of its truth.

"It was such a darn wonderful show in the half dark, I didn't want to miss it," he said. "It sure was pretty to watch those rockets and flares and the artillery flashing way off. I turned back to get another look at it while I had the chance."

Beauty on a battlefield, and a man shoving a plane back into a night sky that might spew death upon him at any moment for another look at it!

Another time he broke out at mess with:

"Gee! You ought to see the fireworks around those balloons! The Huns have a short mortar gun that shoots a string of flaming balls—you know, those flaming onion things. They can't hurt you. They only go up about a thousand feet and fall back. I went back in again so they'd send up some more near me. They look like those flower-pots we used to have on the Fourth of July."

Ask any flier what he thought of the German "flaming onions," then consider how much that going back meant to Luke.

But, with one balloon to his credit, there was no stopping him. Two days after his first victory, he and Wehner were ordered to attack a balloon near Buzy.

Luke got it, while Joe Wehner fought off a formation of eight Fokkers. Then Frank soared off on his own and downed another balloon.

VIII

CAPTAIN GRANT, sprawled over an operations map, addressed Frank Luke, who was following closely a pencil with which the Captain made neat circles around the names of towns. When the Squadron Commander spoke, his tone was that of a man aggrieved.

"Corps has just given Group hell about a drachen [balloon] over near Buzy," he said, "and Hartney has passed the Hades on to me. I'm handing it down to you. Get that sausage and get it today. You can take one man with you. Who do you want?"

"Joe Wehner."

Grant nodded. He sensed something of the friendship between these two.

"All right," he said.

The thrice-qualified balloon probably would cost him one of the pilots, perhaps both; but Corps had demanded it, and Luke was a balloon man if ever there was one.

"Drop out of the formation at Buzy," Grant continued, "and—try to get back. Another thing, Luke: keep your eye peeled, because there's a whole flock of Fokkers nesting under that sausage."

Five minutes later the flight was up, its wings sun-painted for a moment as it squared off for its afternoon patrol over the lines. As the wedge of war birds neared Buzy, Luke wiggled his flippers and swung away from the formation, Wehner following immediately and making altitude.

Wehner was to ride the sun—remain high aloft, using the sun's brilliance as a screen—while Luke worked low on the balloon. In the event of an attack on the balloon strafer by enemy planes, Wehner could zoom down upon the attackers—a fire-spitting avenger from out the fiery orb.

If not too busily engaged with the sausage, Luke would participate in the dogfight certain to follow; but it was ten to one Wehner would have to fight it out alone.

The balloon at Buzy occupied Luke only a few seconds. A long, straight dive, a burst from both guns that pierced the rolls of gassy fat where the rudder-like aftersection bulged, a pall of flame-shot, odorous smoke. That was all.

But the Fokkers had seen him! The entire enemy flight—eight planes—swooped down on his lone machine. He sagged back on the stick, stood the quivering Spad on its tail, and reached for his guns. Jammed!

The Hun leader veered off and up, fell over into perfect attack position, and sprayed him with tracers. Behind him two other Germans were raking his fuselage with short, quick bursts. Bullets splintered his instrument board, fashioned an openwork pattern in his wings. He rolled, tipped the Spad over on one wing, and swung away. Then he saw Wehner.

Throttle open, guns chattering, his goggled face poked far over the edge of the cockpit, Wehner was charging the enemy formation. He dived upon it from above, into it, through it to the planes on Luke's tail. They veered, forgot Luke, and shied off to meet this new menace.

Luke's air position was such that he could not read Wehner's plane markings, and for the moment he thought he was another foe speeding to the attack. Frank's guns were useless, so he availed himself of the temporary respite occasioned by Wehner's onslaught to speed away.

Luke repaired his guns and headed in the direction the formation had taken. Wehner overtook him. They picked up the formation, continuing the patrol until the flight was over Abaucourt, where Luke again left it. He had spotted an enemy balloon near Boinville.

Six times he dived on the unwieldy bag, scorning the tempest of steel that lashed about him. Twice he pulled away, tinkered deliberately with his jammed guns, and returned to the assault.

At Luke's first attack the balloon observer, armed with a light machine gun, fired blindly at the plane roaring down upon him, then abandoned the defense and jumped. Frank didn't want him; but an Archie battery, banging away below, annoyed him. With only seventy-five rounds left in one gun, he dived and strafed it.

His guns empty, but with a scattered battery and a collapsed observation balloon to mark where he had emptied them, he again piloted a bullet-pocked plane back to the Twenty-seventh's landing field.

That night Captain Grant perused Luke's combat report with keen interest. It read:

COMBAT REPORT—*September 14, 1918.*
Lieutenant Frank Luke reports:

I and Lieutenant Wehner were to leave with formation to attack enemy balloon by order of C. O. On arriving at Buzy, left formation and brought down enemy balloon in flames. While fixing my guns so I could attack another balloon near by, eight enemy Fokkers dropped down on me. Pulled away from them. They scored several good shots on my plane.

I saw Lieutenant Wehner dive through enemy formation and attack two enemy planes on my tail; but, as my guns were jammed, did not turn, as I was not sure it was an Allied plane until he joined me later. You will find attached confirmation of balloon.

Left formation at Abaucourt and attacked an enemy balloon near Boinville. Dove at it six times at close range. Had two stoppages with left gun which carried incendiary bullets and, after fixing both, continued the attack. After about seventy-five rounds being left in right gun, I attacked an Archie battery at the base of the balloon. Am sure that my fire took effect as the crews scattered.

After my first attack on the balloon the observer jumped after he shot at me. The last I saw of the balloon, it was on the ground in a very flabby condition. Confirmation requested.

"Why didn't you get that observer?" Luke was asked. His reply was sterling proof of sportsmanship.

"Hell," he said, "the poor devil was helpless!"

Because of Frank's magnanimity, Sergeant Muenchhoff of German Balloon Company No. 14 lived to tell of his effort to bring the Balloon Buster down. According to Muenchhoff's version, Signaler Gasser jumped from the basket a few seconds later. Although both floated slowly earthward, offering excellent targets for Luke's guns, he made no attempt to fire upon them.

With his twin victories on September 14, only two days after he had downed his first balloon, Luke began to take on the stature of the great.

There was a congratulatory message from the Group Commander to top off the fulsome praise of his squadron mates. Wehner, too, became aware of a changed attitude in his brother officers, a new friendliness he would have accepted eagerly in the days when he was regarded as a spy suspect.

Neither of them needed it now. They were combat men, destined to be aces—superaces—within a matter of days at their present pace, and they were sufficient unto themselves.

Luke spent long hours going over his plane, taking up a half-turn on this turnbuckle, easing off a quarter of an inch on that wire. From other hangars and other planes he purloined sundry attachments, small parts and gadgets he believed would add to the fighting and maneuvering ability of his Spad.

In this respect he became a squadron pest; but, because they were aware of the enthusiasm for conquest that prompted these raids, the victimized pilots viewed them with good-humored resignation. As one of them complained to Captain Grant: "It's got so you have to sleep in your ship if you want to keep the damn thing in one piece!"

On September 15 Luke and Wehner were instructed to bring down a German balloon sighted over Boinville. They did not leave their airdrome until after the patrol was up, and then, instead of making the dual attack as ordered, they separated.

Disobedience of orders? Certainly. Rank insubordination, punishable by a general court-martial. Almost any soldier who prides himself on waging war according to the military textbooks would froth at the mouth over such conduct. But consider what that breach of instructions accomplished: Wehner got a balloon and two planes; Luke shot down two balloons!

Northeast of Verdun, Wehner spied a balloon, dropped on it, cindered it with 100 rounds of incendiary ammunition, and crowded his machine into immediate flight with a formation of five enemy planes on his tail. He lost them over Chambley when a formation of French Spads swung in to give battle.

Wehner, remembering a drachen he had seen over the Bois d'Hingry, turned in that direction. When about a mile away he saw it go down in flames and concluded correctly that Luke had shot it down; then he turned south, where he had sighted another sausage. Observing a barrage of antiaircraft in the vicinity of the Bois d'Hingry balloon, Wehner accepted it as an indication that Luke was in difficulties there and sped toward the shrapnel puffs.

Above Rouvrois a plane separated itself from the mist and smoke. It was Luke. With his nose down for speed, he was coming like a bat out of hell, with seven Hun planes booming along behind him. Wehner got one, a Fokker, before the Germans realized he was part of the show. It fell off in a spiral, sideslipped, then spun to the ground.

Joe had bested it as part of his original attack maneuver, so it was only a matter of seconds before his guns, for once functioning perfectly, were streaming tracers into an Albatross close on Luke's tail. It turned, but soon went into a steep dive and crashed.

Wehner swung in behind Luke and both peaked for the American lines. The Hun formation followed until it encountered Allied antiaircraft fire, then turned back. A balloon and two planes for Wehner! Two balloons for Luke! An aërial hare-and-hounds chase over the smoke-dimmed, embattled land that was turned to his advantage only by the participation of Wehner, and he reported it all in thirty-eight words!

Listen to this:

Lieutenant Frank Luke reports:

I left formation and attacked an enemy balloon at Boinville in accordance with instructions and destroyed it. I fired 125 rounds. I then attacked another balloon near Bois d'Hingry and fired fifty rounds into it. Two confirmations requested.

And he wanted more! Again that afternoon he took the air—after the formation, as usual. Let his own combat report tell the story of that third balloon in one day.

COMBAT REPORT—*September 15, 1918.*
Lieutenant Frank Luke reports:

Patrolled to observe enemy activity. Left a little after formation, expecting to find it on the lines. On arriving there I could not find formation but saw artillery firing on both sides. Also saw a light at about 500 meters. At first I thought it was an observation machine but on nearing it I found that it was a Hun balloon, so I attacked and destroyed it. I was Archied with white fire, and machine guns were very active. Returned very low. Saw thousands of small lights in woods north of Verdun. On account of darkness coming on I lost my way and landed in a French wheat field at Agers about twenty-one hours thirty [9:30 P.M.]. Balloon went down in flames at nineteen hours fifty [7:50 P.M.].

Official German records, incomplete in many instances because of the rapidity of the German retreat during the latter days of the war, disclose that Luke was well known to the enemy as early as September 15. They list his victories of that day in detail.

In one of the enemy reports, Lieutenant Wenzel, who used his parachute to escape from Luke's attack, described how the Balloon Buster destroyed one strategically placed bag that had lived through innumerable attacks by French, English, Belgian, and American fliers. This was a drachen in Balloon Company Eighteen of Balloon Battalion Thirty-three.

It was Frank's first victory that day.

Luke returned by motor to an airdrome that buzzed and hummed with the recounting of his exploits. An American balloon company had seen his third burning drachen flaming redly in the night sky, had heard his motor whining overhead, and reported another Yank air conquest to Group Headquarters. The squadron gave the credit to Luke before he arrived to claim it.

Wehner was the first to take his hand when he came in. A spy congratulating a liar! Wehner, who had shot down two balloons and three combat planes in three days. Luke, who had cleared the skies of six enemy balloons in the same period—a record never equaled.

Spy and liar!

Not now! You should have heard that smoke-blued mess room. The clink of bottles and glasses, the scuff of sturdy boots, a mild bedlam of excited voices.

"Tell us about it, Frank! Was there much Archie over d'Hingry? Were there machine guns in any of the baskets? Shut up, damn it, and listen! Were you shot up badly, Joe? Oh, for God's sake, put down the bottle and give somebody else a chance!"

That and its like for an hour. Liar and spy? Why, that squadron would have closed a man's throat with his own smashed teeth if he had dared breathe it. Aces—that's what they were, aces! Men who would be dead within the week consumed with admiration or with envy—as though it mattered!

Messages! Flight commanders and squadron commanders burning telephone wires for a brief "Good work," or "Splendid," or "Tell 'em to leave one balloon for a sample." A side car rattling up to the door, a smart orderly, and, "Group Commander's compliments, sir. He is proud —" Oh, that bronze for their chests was well on its way now!

On the morning of September 16 Luke and Wehner again patrolled the front, but, other than for the evidences of strife below them, they might have been flying over farming land at home. The German balloon line had become wary. Twice they sighted German balloons, and twice the bags were hastily lowered before they could approach within range.

That afternoon Luke went to the Group Commander. To Major Hartney and the Group Operations Officer, Lieutenant Romer Shawhan, he said: "I think I can get a bunch of these Hun balloons with very little risk if you will consider a suggestion I'd like to make. As you know, I got down all right night before last and last night, and Wehner and I now know the sector like a book. As a result of our scouting today we know where we can put our hands on three of them."

He slapped three fingers on the desk.

"How would it be if we left the airdrome just in time to get those balloons at dusk, when their observers are taking a last look at our troop movements? Wehner can get one about seven-ten, I'll get another about seven-twenty, and between us we ought to get the third about seven-thirty. Just start burning flares and shooting rockets here on the drome about that time and we'll get back all right. I'll promise you that."

Major Hartney considered the situation. Could they get back? The landing speed of a Spad was about seventy-five miles an hour—something of a risk under ideal landing conditions; a positive hazard in the dark. Nor was there sufficient time to warn friendly antiaircraft batteries of the contemplated maneuver. Friend and foe alike would strike at them in the dark.

On the other hand, German balloon observation was one of the factors slowing up the St. Mihiel drive, which had commenced September 12.

Hartney's eyes sought those of his Operations Officer. After all, their job was to obtain victories, and if a man pleaded for an opportunity to become more intimately acquainted with death, why not?

"All right," the Major said.

Out came the maps. There is something sinister about the way of strategists with a map. You can almost see their minds function. Here is a small wood—put a machine-gun company in there; that hill offers excellent defilades for artillery; and we can hold this stream with infantry.

I wonder if they ever realized that the machine-gunners, the artillerymen, and the doughboys were just other Toms and Bills and Jacks, down there because they could not all be strategists? They probably never did. It might not add to the success of battles if they came to regard the colored

88

pins in their maps as men who laughed and sang sometimes, when they were happy.

Carefully Luke and his Major went over the aërial map. They weren't placing troops, but they discussed the men who might kill Frank and the men he hoped to kill, in the abstract terms of the staff. From headquarters Luke went to Wehner's billet.

"It's all right, Joe," he said. "Hartney's all for it. Says he'll burn flares and send up rockets so we can get in. We'll take off at six-forty-five. Now, when we get over Verdun—"

Frank and Wehner pored over a small map until notified their planes were warmed up and ready. At 6:45 o'clock to the second Luke nodded, the wheel chocks were yanked free, and they bumped down the field, waving carelessly as they banked over for direction and straightened out toward the line.

The two-man patrol that was to revolutionize balloon combat tactics was on its way.

In front of the Operations Office, Major Hartney, Captain Henry Lyster, and Lieutenant Shawhan, standing in apprehensive silence, stared in the direction the pilots had taken. A short distance away a group of fliers collected, held the darkening sky under close scrutiny, and waited.

The silence thickened. It was the kind of silence in which part of a man's mind counts the buttons on another man's blouse or wonders how many stitches there are in the seam of a riding boot, while the other part toys with suspense and dread and fear born of old experience.

Hartney broke with speech the stillness that soon would have required a yell or a pistol shot.

"It's seven-ten," he said, and in the same breath, "By God, they've got one! Look there!"

They had!

Off to the northeast, beyond Verdun, the sky flared red as though some Gargantuan stove lid had been raised for a few moments, held above the fire box, and slowly replaced. There was quick, animated conversation; then tense, ringing silence. That patrol wasn't back on the drome yet.

At 7:21 o'clock that stove lid was lifted again; again the sky flared red.

"They're a minute late," someone said nervously. A wave of almost hysterical laughter rolled out over the watchers and receded into that tingling silence. But you could feel the strengthened confidence. Two out of three always *was* lucky!

By 7:30 o'clock each man was striving to follow the minute hand of his wrist watch on its labored, halting way and to regard the sky in the region of Verdun at the same time.

7:31—2—3—4—

Hartney coughed nervously and lit a cigarette.

7:35—6—

And he was dashing through the clustered fliers, bellowing:

"There it is! The third one! There it is! Ready with those flares, you men! Get those rockets under way, Shawhan! Lively, now! Burn the damned hangars if you have to, but give 'em a lighted field!"

He scuttled out to meet a gray staff car rolling down to a halt.

"Did you see it, Colonel?" he demanded of the stocky man who was alighting. "Did you see it?"

Indeed Colonel William Mitchell, Chief of Air Service for the First Army, had seen it, for the giant stove lid was slowly descending and cutting off the third red glow as he acknowledged the salutes of the grouped pilots. Years later he spoke of Luke's part in it as "one of the most remarkable feats in the military career of a youngster that was nothing short of amazing."

He said that and more when, a few minutes after his arrival, Luke and Wehner made perfect landings on the light-streaked field. Yes, it worked, they told him, abashed as second lieutenants should be in the presence of a colonel.

The first balloon had given them the least trouble. The sausage swung low over Reville and each flier gave it a long burst from both guns. It flamed up immediately, and they headed for one at Romagne. Luke got that one alone, while Wehner swung off to attack another he had located at Mangiennes.

90

Over Romagne, Frank dived through a curtain of shrapnel to get the bag that was being rapidly lowered by the ground crews. He dropped it upon them, burning, for their pains. He rejoined Wehner, only to leave him and swoop down to strafe a German supply train that had awaited the dusk before starting for the front areas.

Luke again caught up with Wehner, and a few minutes later the American antiaircraft went into action against them, scoring several hits on both planes. To avoid disaster at the hands of men who, the next day, would thrill to the tale of the three balloons, they climbed for a long circle and a swooping descent onto the field.

Within an hour Corps Headquarters was ponderously excited over the astounding success of what it was pleased to describe as "a unique air maneuver by pilots under its command."

By noon the next day the troops had it, for news of the two-man offensive and its results traveled through the battle zone fast.

This guy Luke again, huh? What a baby he must be! Nine victories to his credit, eight of them observation balloons, and the entire eight bagged in five consecutive days!

Thereafter they looked for him, and whenever they saw a lone Spad streaking for the German lines they identified it as Luke's.

"That's Luke," they would say, turning grimed, unshaven faces to the sky. " 'Atta boy! Go get 'em, Arizona! Ride 'em, cowboy!"

And Luke rode 'em—for the thirteen days he had to live!

IX

TO almost everyone who participated in it, the war brought at least one new and consuming ambition. One man might desire military rank above all other things; another would dedicate his life to a search for the enemy of mankind who abolished a hat in favor of the collapsible, folding monkey bonnet, which created in the minds of modest men a painful sensation of not being suitably clothed for public gaze.

At least once in the life of every combat soldier the yearning for the deepest corner of the deepest dugout ever constructed made all other desires seem cheap and unworthy.

Frank Luke's war-born desire was to capture a German airplane with its machine guns intact. He wanted them not only because they would serve as mementos of combats in the air, but for other reasons as well.

"You can't tell," he would say, when asked why he wished to burden himself with such cumbersome souvenirs. "Maybe there'll be another revolution in Mexico and we'll need 'em in Arizona. Maybe"—and here his eyes would twinkle—"I'll start one myself when I get back!"

Although he did not have the opportunity to take the guns from an enemy he personally had destroyed, he got them September 17, the day after he and Joe Wehner had put on their first twilight balloon strafe.

St. Mihiel had fallen, and Frank forsook flying for one day to motor into the war-trampled territory he had helped take by his interference with enemy observation. Ahead of him the crest of battle still formed and broke, surged and formed and broke again in olive-drab avalanches over the retreating Germans. The Allies were on the other end of the chase and they liked it!

Frank found his guns behind the front wall of what once had been a home. Here such important matters as whether to plant one or two rows of chives in the garden had been decided; here neighbors had been talked about; here a daughter had become betrothed; and here a rosary had been fervently uttered for a son who spent too many hours with a woman who had no shame.

Upstairs, babies had wailed their way into life and wrinkled grandmothers and grandfathers had mumbled their way out. Now it housed half a dozen dead Germans and a pair of machine guns.

The litter of war—a dented canteen, a shrapnel-split helmet, and a well-oiled belt—scorned by rats who had choicer morsels—lay about. Upstairs— There was no upstairs. The sky came next, and it should have been a source of gratitude that there was no roof to shut a man in with the inmates.

Frank loaded the machine guns into the squadron car and returned to the airdrome, where he and Joe Wehner spent the remainder of the afternoon cleaning and polishing them. Frank packed the weapons in specially constructed cases and shipped them back to Paris to be held for him.

This episode of the machine guns pleased Luke, and mechanics overheard him still discussing them as he and Wehner walked out to their planes the next afternoon.

They flew alone. After that demonstration of September 16, they could have flown the commanding officer's motor car if they had wanted to. Over St. Mihiel they sighted two balloons above Labeuville, and Luke climbed swiftly, sure of at least one more balloon for his score.

It was getting to be old business, this making altitude, giving the instruments a last quick reading, then tipping into a full-throttled dive that always seemed about to strip the wings of their canvas.

Old, yet ever new. The balloon rushing up never came

at just the same angle, the chocolate cream puffs splattering the air wove a different pattern each time, and the observers always behaved differently.

Sometimes they jumped early, swinging out like tiny pendulums under their parachutes. Sometimes they didn't jump at all, but, dictated to by supreme courage or terror, stuck to their baskets and went down in the flaming gas!

Luke registered on the higher balloon first. He was down where the enemy Archie batteries didn't dare fire before he put in his first burst.

That was all he needed. The sausage gave a great red sigh and collapsed. He leveled off, came up and over, rolled and made for the other drachen, spattered it with both guns, and banked off as it puffed out in a burst of crimson and black.

Where was Joe?

Frank had expected him to take the second sausage. Maybe—

He jerked back on the stick and the Spad sag-tailed under him. Wehner was above him, and perilously close on his tail was a formation of Fokkers!

They were close-wedged and coming fast—beautiful, but Luke needed no vision other than his own to see a mess of blackened metal and the raw earth of a new grave beyond that beauty.

As Frank made altitude, the formation split, the main body crowding Wehner while two attacked him from the rear. The Hun in the lead committed the fatal blunder of sacrificing the altitude that would have given him victory and continued his dive to Luke's level.

The latter made for him with both guns going. Only the German's death in the air prevented a head-on collision between those two planes. There were but a few yards between them when the Hun turned, fell into a nose dive that became an erratic tail spin, and crashed.

The Arizonian swung on the second German, felt his Spad quiver under a quick, hot burst from the enemy's guns, and shot him into a dive. Fearful that he had lost too much altitude and would be easy prey for others in the

Hun formation, he banked for altitude and saw them milling above him.

Wehner was gone; so, believing Joe had seized upon his arrival as an opportunity to peak for home, Frank made for the American lines.

Turning east at the Allied balloon line, Luke saw a friendly antiaircraft barrage ahead of him and made for it. Allied Archie meant an enemy raider! Southeast of Verdun he saw a German observation plane being pursued by a squadron of Spads. Not until later did he learn that they were his friends the Cigognes, whose type of planes had been changed.

Having an advantageous position, he whipped in ahead of the pursuers, squared away for position, lined his sights on the pilot's cockpit, and let him have both guns. The German plane kicked up on its side, trembled, tipped, and burned a wavering course earthward.

Two combat planes, two balloons, one observation plane, and it was less than ten minutes since he and Wehner had started their dives on the sausages at Labeuville! If we had all stayed home and knit shoestrings, we could flick our coat tails in the face of the world because of that one American's feat of arms.

Three planes and two balloons in less than ten minutes! Hell's bells, man, you couldn't tell a more astounding story if you had until next Christmas to make it up!

As Luke turned away after his fifth victory—the Halberstadt observation plane—his petrol gave out. He switched on the *nourrice*—"nursemaid" is the literal translation—a ten-minute supply of gasoline carried in the superior wing of a Spad.

With this emergency fuel he made a safe landing below Verdun, not far from where the Halberstadt had crashed. There was a good flying field there that had been abandoned by the French because the Germans had perfect artillery registered on it.

The enemy was striving desperately to prevent Allied planes from basing on advanced flying fields, as secret reports to the German chief commander of the air show, and they were concentrating about Verdun.

These same reports disclose also that Frank added a touch of almost unbelievable daring to his September 18 combat by descending to within ninety feet of the ground to get his second balloon that day.

In their combat reports to the German High Command, Lieutenant Finster and Lieutenant Heicke of Balloon Company 112, Balloon Battalion Twenty, and Lieutenant Roerich of the protecting antiaircraft artillery testified that Frank's Spad was within that distance of the ground when the big bag burst into flames.

From the Verdun landing field Frank hastened back to the Twenty-seventh airdrome in a borrowed side car. He wanted to get further details of the dogfight from Joe and tell him about the Halberstadt. He made a verbal report at headquarters, asked to have his ship flown back, and was turning to leave when Major Hartney spoke to him:

"Luke, I'm sorry—" he began, but Frank interrupted him.

"D'you mind if I dash along, Major?" he asked. "I'll be back with my combat report as soon as I get those confirmations from Joe."

Hartney let him go.

There was a whistle and a slammed door—certain evidences of good humor in Frank Luke. At Wehner's billet he kicked open the door and called:

"Hey, Joe!"

Receiving no answer, he stepped across the threshold for a look about the room. Empty. There were other pilots in the building who knew about Wehner, but there are certain things even a brave man cannot do.

Frank next looked for him at the hangars. One of Wehner's mechanics, as burly a wrench-swinger as ever pulled on a suit of dungarees, stood up as Luke entered the shelter where Joe usually garaged his plane.

"Where's Lieutenant Wehner?" Frank asked, and read his answer in the tear-streaked grime on the mechanician's face.

"They—they got him in that God-damned dogfight!" the ground man said in a broken voice, and his shoulders heaved. Ever see a horse-muscled, physically capable man cry? Well, don't watch one. It isn't pretty.

It was then that Frank Luke gathered the knowledge that the taste of defeat is bitter—more bitter than childhood medicine; and it was in that minute—and that minute only—he knew what it was to be whipped! Whipped without raising a hand, because here was a thing you couldn't punch or shoot or throttle.

"But maybe he's only missing," Frank said. God in heaven! Does the combat officer live who hasn't gone on mumbling, "Maybe he's only missing! Maybe he's only missing!" until someone has stumbled over the crumpled body in the dark?

"Aw, we can't kid ourselves!" the mechanic snarled. "Some of them frog Cigognes saw him go down in flames over Labeuville. Why the hell didn't they go in and shoot the guts out of them Heinies, if they could see so well? I'd like to get my hands on just one of that Hun formation, the dirty, lousy—"

He went back to his tools sobbing profanities that seemed flat and inadequate. Luke left the hangar for— where? There wasn't any place to go. Joe Wehner was dead! Down in flames over Labeuville! Not again would he hear that voice, a voice he had come to listen for:

"Howdy, boy! Let's go get us a balloon!"

Somebody passed him—Ivan Roberts—snapped him an exaggerated salute, and called:

"Great stuff, Frank! Five at a time. 'Atta boy!"

What the hell did he mean, "great stuff," with Joe Wehner down in flames over Labeuville? Why, yesterday at this time—only yesterday, twenty-four hours ago—Joe was sitting opposite him, rubbing down one of those souvenir German machine guns with an oily rag.

They were laughing, too. Frank always laughed when Joe was around. Things he said were funny. They wouldn't be funny if other fellows said them, but when Joe said them—well, you just had to laugh.

And was he game? Tell the cockeyed world he was! Game as they make 'em. "You get 'em, Frank. I'll ride the sun," he would say. That was old Joe, all right. And he'd taken it on the nose from those bomb-proof spy chasers, too. Never squawked once, either. What it took to make a man, Joe sure had. Only yesterday in that dogfight—Wehner down in flames over Labeuville!

Aimlessly Luke moved about the field, lost among familiar objects. Men passed him, saw his face, and withheld a greeting. They, too, once had friends with whom they had laughed. Friends who had come down in flames over some God-forgotten huddle in a field afar.

He went to his quarters. At this time every day he went to his quarters. The night came in to cover him sitting there on his cot. Feet moved in the corridor and a low voice asked:

"Going to chow, Frank?"

No answer. Against the gloom there was a tensed blur that was Frank Luke. The feet moved away softly and, somehow, the owner was conscious that there were no tears there in the dark. Frank wasn't the crying kind.

Could he have wept then, sobbed out his hurt as that grimed mechanic had in a welter of tears that cleanses a man, he might have lived more than eleven days. But tears were a weakness and, by all eternal things, he *couldn't* cry with Joe Wehner down in flames over Labeuville!

Outside a bugle sent shafts of brassy melody into the night and Frank turned on his light. He had forgotten. There was a war and he had shot down some airplanes in it and there was a combat—*Joe Wehner down in flames over Labeuville*—report he had—*down in flames over Labeuville*—to give to—*Joe Wehner down*—Major Hartney.

His report finished, he sent it to the Major by an orderly. The Group Commander took it eagerly, read it with avid interest, for he knew then that it was a document which would attract the eyes of men in generations to come—the pilot's own account of the world's greatest single achievement in aërial warfare.

It read:

COMBAT REPORT—*September 18, 1918.*

Lieutenant Frank Luke reports:

Lieutenant Wehner and I left the airdrome at sixteen

98

hours [4 P. M.] to spot enemy balloons. Over St. Mihiel we saw two German balloons near Labeuville. Maneuvered in the clouds and dropped down, burning both. We were then attacked by a number of E. A. [enemy aircraft], the main formation attacking Lieutenant Wehner, who was above and on one side. I started climbing to join the fight when two E. A. attacked me from the rear. I turned on them, opening both guns on the leader. We came head on until within a few yards of each other when my opponent turned to one side in a nose dive and I saw him crash to the ground.

I then turned on the second, shot a short burst, and he turned and went into a dive. I saw a number of E. A. above but could not find Lieutenant Wehner, so turned and made for our lines. The above fight occurred in the vicinity of St. Hilaire. On reaching our balloon line, flew east. Saw Archie on our side, flew toward it, and found an enemy observation machine. I gave chase with some other Spads and got him off from his lines. After a short encounter he crashed within our lines, southeast of Verdun. Lieutenant Wehner is entitled to share in the victories over both the balloons. Confirmations requested, two balloons and three planes.

The confirmations came in, all of them. Frank Luke was now the leading ace in the American air service. Rickenbacker the mighty was five victories behind him. Luke had a total of fourteen victories: four planes and ten balloons.

But the truly amazing feature of this record is that thirteen of his conquests were won in a single week, during which there were two days—September 13 and September 17—on which he did not fly. On the eighteenth alone he had bested five of his enemies.

Late that night, General Pershing took from an aide's hand a military telegraph form and focused tired eyes on one sentence:

Second Lieutenant Frank Luke, Jr., Twenty-seventh Aero Squadron, First Pursuit Group, five confirmed victories, two combat planes, two observation balloons, and one observation plane in less than ten minutes.

Not a word about Joe Wehner, but that was as it should be. Generals do not count their dead, only their victories.

There would be medals, of course—bronze for the chest of the premier ace, who, a month before, had been branded a liar!

Frank was the greatest combat flier America had given the world. He had come to his high place. It found him sitting silently on a cot in a darkened room, denied the benison of tears, and he needed them because Joe Wehner had gone down in flames over Labeuville.

X

WE have been told that wartime Paris was a wicked city, but many who passed that way during the red years did not know it as that. There was a Paris that winked slyly at you, took you to one side, and whispered:

"See here, old lad, just because you've had a tough time of it you mustn't sit around and sulk."

She signaled the musicians, beckoned to her prettiest women, filled your glass, and told you not to be silly. Of course there wasn't a war—you'd just dreamed it. And, by George, you began to believe you had!

Intelligent commanding officers knew these things and, where possible, when young men of attainments took too frequently to the bottle, or just stared, stared, stared with nothing to stare at, they wrote out a pass, loaned them money if necessary, and packed them off to Paris with a muttered prayer that they would not become entirely sane and refuse to return.

When, after Joe Wehner's death, Frank Luke sat staring, staring, staring at vivid scenes the others could not see, but one remedy suggested itself—leave to Paris.

In the French capital he would forget the things he should forget. At least they would become blurred, indistinct, so he could live with them and retain his reason.

There would be women to help him forget. Not the grizzled, mustached *femmes de guerre* of the Second Empire, but soft, warm, gay creatures who took haggard young men, cold and tired after a walk with death along the shell-lashed ways that led to the whipping post of battle, and found a lost sparkle for eyes gone lusterless from regarding dead and shattered things.

"Take us," they said. "Laugh and dance and drink with us, for tomorrow you may die!"

Battle men took them eagerly, hungrily, hurriedly—for troop trains move on schedule and war is a jealous mistress.

Oh, yes, some of it was sordid prostitution; but those blind ones who hold all of the fleeting loves of men at war under this classification commit sacrilege; and any man who has lived in hunger and filth and fear for days, to crawl back to the warmth of a woman's arms, will tell you so!

Frank Luke came to a Paris that was unusually, artificially gay. Like a girl who, snubbed at her first party, seeks to hide the hurt by laughing too shrilly.

Paris had hurts to hide. In the early days of the war she had gone suddenly silent, a city living in suspended animation, a capital of gayety still as a young nun before an altar. No lights winked on the Seine. The heights of the Trocadéro were ominously somber. The echoing boulevards were still.

But in September, 1918? You'll never look upon its like again—you who saw it then! For four years the Hun had blustered and brawled at the very gates of the city.

Now that he was in retreat, Paris rouged her cheeks, threw a mantle of light, gay laughter over her mourning, and went out to dance in the streets.

She found a reluctant dancing partner in Frank Luke. On every hand women spoke to him seductively—some shyly, but none the less eloquently, with young eyes grown old too soon; others brazenly, commandingly, with gestures and with words that never yet have required an interpreter.

Frank paused with none of them, not because he did not have the desires of other men, but because he had no room for thought of such things.

Joe Wehner had gone down in flames over Labeuville and, until there had been some adjustment of that calamity he could think of nothing else.

Had he got filthy drunk, wallowed, broken a trust, and

hurt a friend or two, to suffer back to normal, sober things under the lashes of shame and humiliation, he might have served himself well. Might, I say, because in this way he could have burned his emotions down to a new beginning, precisely his greatest need.

Had he found a companion—any companion to talk to him about anything—the end might have arranged itself differently.

Isn't there true pathos in that picture of Frank Luke, sent to Paris to find and partake of the city's blood-bought gayety, moving through it with unseeing eyes? He—the boy once regarded as the life of the party, the grinning young hellion who blew in on a gale of laughter and kept the breeze blowing—lost in the world's gayest party.

When his leave was only half over he returned to his squadron and immediately after reporting went in search of Major Hartney.

"You're back early, aren't you?" asked Hartney.

"Yes, sir," Luke responded.

With a list as long as his arm of pilots A. W. O. L. because of the delights of Paris, Hartney could not understand a man who voluntarily forfeited half of his leave.

"Why?" he asked.

"There wasn't anything to do," explained Frank, and saw no reason for his Major's amazement. But Luke had not returned to sit about and brood. His next sentence proved that.

"Major," he said, "remember that old frog drome I landed on the day—the day I got three planes?"

"Yes," responded the Group Commander, interested as a soldier now.

"Well," Luke went on, "if you'll put a flight up there we can raise hell with the German balloon line. More than that, too. It's ten miles nearer the front and we can get their bombers and observation planes a few minutes after the front lines spot 'em. I'd like to go up with that flight."

"But the place has been shelled flat a dozen times," Hartney argued.

Luke waved this aside with a gesture.

"I know that," he said. "But it hasn't been used in

103

months, the hangars are in fair shape, and we can get in some good work before they shell us out. If you don't want to send a flight up, Major, let me go alone. Please, let me try it."

Once before Luke had talked in that vein and the greatest two-man balloon offensive in aërial history had resulted. Once before Hartney had considered one of Luke's daring propositions only to arrive at the conclusion that his job was to get victories, not safeguard individuals.

"All right," the Major said.

The flight moved up under the command of Jerry Vasconcelles, the captain whose praise of pilots who voluntarily attacked balloons had launched Luke on his balloon-busting career.

If Frank was elated over the acceptance of his suggestion, it was not displayed in his manner. He was blunt, taciturn. A terse reticence crept into the letter he wrote his mother on September 25—his last letter home. It follows:

September 25, 1918.

Dear Mother:

I have not written for some days now on account of being so busy, as no doubt you have already heard. This is only a line to let you know that I am O. K. Now, mother, remember that I have passed the dangerous stage of being a new hand at the game, so don't worry, for I now know how to take care of myself.

Love to all,
FRANK.

No word of Joe Wehner. No attempt to tell with honest, deserved pride of his victories. No pouring of himself on paper, that the one who always had soothed his hurts might know and comfort him from afar. He could not find expression even for his mother, and when a man becomes that self-contained there is a bad fall and a reckoning at the end of the road.

Frank continued to regard himself as a balloon buster, and merely awaited the assignment of a flying mate to continue the twilight assaults he and Wehner had inaugurated.

Lieutenant Ivan A. Roberts of South Lee, Massachusetts, was detailed to fly with him, and on September 26 they made their first dual flight. Frank bolstered his score with a victory over an enemy combat plane, a conquest he describes tersely in the ensuing report:

COMBAT REPORT—*September 26, 1918.*
Lieutenant Frank Luke reports:

On patrol to strafe balloons in vicinity Consenvoye and Sivry I attacked with two others [a third plane had joined them after they left the airdrome] a formation of five Fokkers. After firing several short bursts, observed the Hun go down out of control. While at 100 meters [328 feet] I was attacked by two E. A. [enemy aircraft] so I did not see the first E. A. crash.

I turned on the other two who were on my tail, getting on the tail of one, but guns jammed several times and after fixing both could only shoot short bursts on account of the several stoppages. One confirmation requested. The last I saw of Lieutenant Roberts, who was on this patrol with me, was in combat with several Fokkers in the vicinity of Consenvoye and Sivry.

The fate of Lieutenant Roberts is obscured with conjecture and rumor. He was seen to crash in German territory, but thereafter no authentic chronicle of his movements is available. Late in 1920 Captain Grant received at his Los Angeles home the following letter, addressed to the Secretary, American Legion, New York City:

DEAR SIR:

Please to forward the following information to the family of Lieut. Ivan A. Roberts.

Lieut. Roberts on the evening of Sept. 25th [should be September 26], 1918, rolled, engine trouble to ground about 12 kilos east of Sivry. On the morning of Sept. 26th, 1918, he was picked up with lacerated scalp and slightly wrenched hip by H. M. Prussian Guard, 42nd Squad.

On Oct. 2nd, 1918, he arrived at the place where I was held prisoner, a temporary structure on Murg River in Baden about 50 kilos from Sackingen. I will not detail our experiences.

On Oct. 7th Lieut. Roberts and myself managed to effect our successful escape leaving three of His Majesty's Prus. G's in the Murg. However, Roberts sustained a bad cut running from ear to collar bone.

We travelled westerly to the Rhine River and northward to Strassbourg. We were subsequently arrested by two men on horseback who had probably observed our departure from the house. After the little "difficulty" there was one horse standing. We both mounted and travelled for Nancy. After perhaps three hours travelling, the horse stepped in an old well and Roberts pulled me out, rather done for, don't you know?

We layed around the well, until the twelfth of Oct. and resumed our way toward Nancy. Roberts' temperature jumped to "top" and he became uncomfortably talkative in view of our close proximity to village homes. Of course we had no medicine of any description. Had I thought there was any degree of salvation for Roberts in surrendering him I should have done so. But as I knew we were wanted real bad and in view of my past experiences I decided to do for us, myself, what I could and which was pitiably little indeed.

We arrived at a small densely wooded cañon about noon on October 14th. We were about 5 kilos from a small and beautiful place called Wasselbonne. We climbed to the bottom of the cañon. Roberts insisted upon bathing his feet despite his physical condition. So it was there, near Wasselbonne, in the cañon laying with his burning head in my dampened jacket, and his feet dangling in the pool, that Ivan offered up a few trinkets and a letter to my care to be taken home. I did the best I could with rocks, limbs, etc., a heartache and a big lump in my throat.

The Lieutenant's little personal things together with my own are at present en route from Paris, where I left them with a friend. I will forward them upon receipt of address. Please treat this letter as it is given. In confidence as I have no desire for notoriety. I am sick of it all and trying to forget. Also pardon mistakes, grammatical, etc., as I am anything but well.

Sincerely,
JACK LA GRANGE, M.D.

The American Legion has no record of a Dr. Jack La Grange, nor has Captain Grant ever been able to locate the writer of the letter.

The German plane Frank shot down the day Roberts spun in and out of control was piloted by Lieutenant J. von Ziegesar, commanding officer of Jagdstaffel Fifteen. Lieutenant von Ziegesar, according to his own combat report, was able to pull his ship out of its nose dive a few moments before reaching the ground behind the German lines, and landed safely. He claims to have recognized his opponent as the feared Balloon Buster.

When Frank learned that Lieutenant Roberts was missing in action under circumstances similar to those in the case of Joe Wehner, he again secluded himself in his quarters. The next day, September 27, he absented himself from the squadron without permission and drew a scathing reprimand.

Smarting under the verbal disciplining, yet unchastened by it, Frank took his Spad up for an unauthorized flight and swooped so low over Bantheville that he burned a partly inflated balloon in its nest.

Scornful of an antiaircraft barrage that would have endangered the flight of a swallow, he spiraled aloft and made for the landing field of his friends, the Cigognes. He remained there that night, returning to the Twenty-seventh's airdrome the next day.

"The skipper wants you," his mechanics informed him gravely when he taxied in. He went directly to Squadron Headquarters.

"Where were *you* last night, Luke?" his captain demanded.

"Cigognes," Frank replied bluntly, adding, as he flipped his combat report on Grant's desk, "There's another balloon. I got it over near Bantheville."

Grant spoke sternly:

"See here, Luke. You're a good flier, one hell of a good flier, and you're also the damnedest nuisance that ever stepped upon a flying field. But you're not running this outfit. Understand that! And you'll conform as the others

107

do. You're on the ground until further notice. D'ye hear that?"

Luke heard, saluted, banged the door, and strode back to his plane.

"She's short o' gas 'n' oil," a mechanic warned him as he climbed into the cockpit.

Luke nodded. "I'll fill her at Vasconcelles' flight at Verdun," he said, blipped his motor on full, and hung her up on the propeller.

Captain Grant was still regarding Luke's combat report when an orderly announced the Arizonian's take-off for Verdun. Grant turned to his adjutant.

"Telephone Jerry to place him under arrest when he gets there," the Squadron Commander ordered. "Say I'll send a pilot up to fly the ship home. Luke can come back in the side car."

The adjutant paused a moment before inquiring:

"What'll you do to him, now?"

For a long minute Grant frowned at his assistant.

"I'm going to recommend him for the Distinguished Service Cross," he said. "Then, by God, I'm going to court-martial him!"

They never convened that court.

Captain Vasconcelles informed Luke of Grant's action as soon as Frank came down on the Verdun field, but their conversation was interrupted by Major Hartney's plane roaring in over their heads.

Vasconcelles, undoubtedly not wishing to take any steps that might conflict with the wishes of his immediate superior, Grant, said nothing of the arrest order that had been issued against Luke.

Hartney had scarcely alighted from his plane when Frank trotted up to him.

"Major," he said quickly, "I know where there are three drachens over by Verdun, and I can get all three of 'em, too, if you'll let me go now!"

Hartney looked at his watch. It was a few minutes after 5 o'clock.

"Too early," he said. "The sun'll drop about five-twenty-two and you can take off then—not before."

108

Frank legged it back to his plane.

"Gas 'er up," he instructed the mechanics. "I got a lotta balloons to get!"

Under arrest, was he? So was Santa Claus! He'd get those sausages, then he'd come back and bust somebody in the nose!

At 5:20 o'clock he signaled the mechanic at his propeller and the Spad thundered into life. Outside, Hartney was encountering difficulties in starting the consumptive Camel the shortage of planes had compelled him to fly. He pushed up his goggles and bellowed profanities at Luke.

"Shut off that motor, you insubordinate such-and-such!" he howled. "I said five-twenty-two, and that means five-twenty-two, you grinning this-and-that!"

Luke switched off his motor and laughed.

"That's the last I remember of him," Hartney told me. "Sitting there in his plane laughing at me while I bawled him out. Lord, what a flier he was—the greatest pilot that ever stepped into a ship!"

At 5:22 o'clock Frank was under way, flying low in the direction of the American balloon headquarters at Souilly. He banked over within spitting range of the headquarters building and tossed a note to a group of surprised observers. It read.

Watch three Hun balloons on the Meuse.   LUKE.

Frank climbed, pointed for Dunsur-Meuse, on the far bank, and swooped down on his first balloon. With guns working perfectly he raked it with cross fire, hung for a moment in a half roll until it belched flame at him, then made for Brière Farm. As he nosed over for his dive, the blunt snout of the second sausage bobbed and nodded for all the world like a mighty football soaring in the arc of a punt. Then he lost it.

Some object thudded against his ribs and he forgot things momentarily.

The Spad trembled, tipped perilously, but righted again as Frank's brain cleared and he found his hands giving instinctive, accustomed service to the controls. He was vaguely conscious that something had happened.

That jolt in the side—

Oh, yes, he had caught the punt! That was it. The other side had kicked off. He was conscious of a movement behind him and knew it would be a teammate sweeping in to take out opposing tackles. Then he realized he was wet—stickily wet—and that a splotch of crimson dirtied his immaculate instrument board.

He was hit!

That movement behind him wasn't a teammate! He should have known all along that it was Joe Wehner diving on a Hun formation.

But Joe Wehner was dead. Down in flames over Labeuville.

He turned, saw the German squadron speeding for place above him, was aware of the flight of their tracers, and threw his Spad into a nose dive. That fooled them. Believing he had crashed, the Huns swerved off for other prey.

Frank leveled his ship, came up under the belly of the Brière Farm balloon, and stabbed it again and again with short bursts of incendiary ammunition.

Flame . . . Smoke . . . A sagging bag . . . Another victory!

Below him the antiaircraft batteries flashed and snorted and puffed—puffed and snorted and flashed. Frank pulled back on the stick, the Spad buck-jumped under him for altitude, and he swung toward Milly, where he had spotted the third balloon.

The badly wounded pilot and his shell-smashed junk heap of a Spad careened drunkenly through a shrapnel-filled dusk toward the third balloon in almost as many minutes.

Although Frank pursued a course marked by what French peasant witnesses later described as incessant fire, he dived unswervingly on the drachen at Milly and destroyed it—his third balloon that day. A total of fourteen balloons and five planes—but it was his final score.

He did not gain altitude again. Perhaps he had bled too profusely, or maybe the Spad was too sorely hurt.

But the motor wasn't whipped. Still roaring defiantly, it propelled the ship in a slanting course toward Murvaux, a small village on the north bank of the Meuse east of Dun.

Luke wasn't through, either.

German troops, like scuttling gray pygmies, filled the principal street as Luke bore down on the town. He unleashed his guns and they spread for cover.

Not all of them, though.

Here and there gray-clad forms stumbled, halted, and crashed to the cobbles or sprawled in grotesque huddles as the steel-jacketed service ammunition plowed through them. He could chalk up six right there for the friend they had robbed him of over Labeuville!

Behind the church on the outskirts of the village, what once had been a lovely meadow sloped down to a small stream.

Sanctuary?

Not there, nor anywhere else in that flame-swept section of a world gone satanic. Why, the cross itself was shrapnel-bruised!

The Spad bumped in, lurched over the uneven ground, and halted. They were down for the last time—Frank and the bullet-belching steed that had cost their enemies one and a half million dollars in balloons and an unnamable sum in shattered morale.

German troops appeared at a fringe of trees bordering the town as Frank slid painfully from the cockpit and started a faltering course for the stream. Something gray bobbed out there in the middle—

A mesquite stump in a stream and a group of shouting men beyond it. Where had he seen that before? Bill Elder. Good old Bill!

"Hold it, Bill, I'm—"

No, it wasn't Bill. Just a dead Hun, face down in the shallow water. But those men at the far side? They were alive enough. He could hear them, shouting:

"Kamerad! Kamerad!"

Kamerad, hell! They shot Joe Wehner down in flames over Labeuville, damn them! He turned back to the Spad, jerking at his automatic. Crouched over the gun, he pushed down the thumb safety and pulled the trigger. The flat crack and the kick of it in his weakened hand was heartening, and he fired again.

111

Again and again and again he squeezed the trigger, using tiny spots of flame in the fringe of trees for targets. Then the darkness came. Frank wilted above the sagging .45, slid along the fuselage of the battered Spad, and crumpled to the ground. He was dead.

XI

MISSING in action!

Among the direful destinations to which a soldier marches, count that the least to be desired. If he is killed, he is killed, and that's an end to it. Those who loved him can do their weeping and go about the business of finding solace gracefully. Being wounded speeds a bath, a shave, and a bed to sleep in. But to be "missing in action" is to inhabit the limbo of war.

He may be on the barbed wire, crucified by the stuff with which men in peacetime safeguard cattle and crops. He may be wallowing in a shell hole, uttering curses at shrapnel that only shattered his legs. He may be in the hands of the enemy, who may be a magnanimous enemy —or who may not.

Wherever he is, he is dead for the missing-in-action period; he is of the grave, yet lacking the cold, gray dignity of a corpse. The counted dead can be buried, the known wounded can be healed—or numbered with the other dead —but a missing-in-action can have none of these services.

Hope springs eternal—in the breasts of mothers 6,000 miles from the battle line and group commanders who need pilots for tomorrow's dawn patrol. Not until the last will they consider him a victim of the fate he is most apt to have encountered—death.

For three months Frank Luke was carried on the rolls as "missing in action."

During the night of September 29, Luke's home field at Rembercourt was marked by the firing of rockets and signal pistols. By noon of September 30, American Balloon Headquarters had confirmed his three victories, but there was no word of Frank.

One of the barbed courtesies of air combat was the custom of dropping a note within the enemy's lines, informing him of the fate of a noteworthy flier. Although there were many cases wherein this service was not rendered, it is entirely possible that Luke's death was not so reported because he did not fall as a result of battle between fighting planes.

As time passed and no word of his arrival in a German prison camp came from the various agencies, official and underground, through which such news traveled, his squadron came reluctantly to regard him as dead.

The Armistice came; the world got drunk, boasted about its hangover, and went back to work. The armies retired to the nameless places where disbanded armies go. New quarrels arose to obliterate the old. And still Frank Luke was missing in action.

Not until January 3, 1919, when the following letter was written, did the American military authorities have definite word of his death:

FROM: Graves Registration Officer, Neufchâteau Area No. 1.

TO: Chief of Air Service, A. P. O. [American Post Office] 717.

SUBJECT: Grave, unknown American aviator.

1. Units of this service have located the grave of an unknown aviator killed on Sunday, September 29, 1918, in the village of Murvaux.

2. From the inspection of the grave and interview held with the inhabitants of this town, the following information was learned in regard to this aviator and his heroism. He is reported as having light hair, young, of medium height, and of heavy stature.

3. Reported by the inhabitants that previous to being killed this man had brought down three German balloons,

114

two German planes, and dropped hand bombs, killing eleven German soldiers and wounding a number of others.

4. He was wounded himself in the shoulder and evidently had to make a forced landing. Upon landing he opened fire with his automatic and fought until he was killed.

5. It is also reported that the Germans took his shoes, leggings, and money, leaving his grave unmarked.

CHESTER E. STATEN,
Captain of Infantry,
G. R. S. Officer.

Although everyone at air headquarters believed this to be Luke's grave, General Pershing personally ordered a General Headquarters staff officer to make an investigation. The Distinguished Service Cross, issued primarily on Captain Grant's recommendation, already awaited Luke, and the Italians desired to confer upon him the Croce di Guerra. The bronze for his chest was accumulating.

The staff officer's report reads:

UNIDENTIFIED AVIATOR

1. This officer was killed at Murvaux (five kilometers east of Dun-sur-Meuse on Sunday, September 29, 1918. The Germans stripped him of all identifications, but Captain McCormick of the Three Hundred and First Unit, Graves Registration, stationed at Fontaine near Murvaux, stated concerning the death of this aviator, that he exhumed the body, that it was a man of medium height, heavy set, and with light hair. On his wrist he found an Elgin watch No. 20225566, which was under the sleeve of his combination and which the Germans had evidently missed. . . .

4. The description of this aviator by Captain McCormick, and the fact that Lieutenant Luke dropped a note to a balloon company that day stating that he was going to shoot down the balloons which were shot down, make it almost certain that this officer was Second Lieutenant Frank Luke, Air Service, whose nearest relative is Frank Luke, 2200 West Monroe Street, Phoenix, Arizona.

5. If the Air Service wishes to check this case it is

suggested that a representative of the Air Service be sent to Murvaux and obtain sworn statements from the French people of that village.

Officers of the Rembercourt Field went to Murvaux, a scant two hours' ride by motor car, and obtained the following sworn statement from some of the citizens of that village:

AFFIDAVIT

The undersigned, living in the town of Murvaux, Department of the Meuse, certify to have seen on the twenty-ninth day of September, 1918, toward evening, an American aviator, followed by an escadrille of Germans, in the direction of Liny, near Dun (Meuse), descend suddenly and vertically toward the earth, then straighten out close to the ground and fly in the direction of the Brière Farm, near Doulcon, where he found a captive balloon, which he burned. Following this he flew toward Milly (Meuse), where he found another balloon, which he also burned, in spite of an incessant fire directed against his machine.

There he was apparently wounded by a shot fired from rapid-fire cannon. From there he came back over Murvaux, and with his machine gun killed six German soldiers and wounded many more.

Following this he landed and got out of his machine, undoubtedly to quench his thirst at a near-by stream. He had gone some fifty yards, when, seeing the Germans come toward him, he still had strength to draw his revolver to defend himself, and a moment after fell dead, following a serious wound received in the chest.

Certify equally to having seen the German commandant of the village refuse to have straw placed in the cart carrying the dead aviator to the village cemetery. This same officer drove away some women bringing a sheet to serve as a shroud for the hero, and said, kicking the body:

"Get that out of my way as quickly as possible."

The next day the Germans took away the airplane, and the inhabitants also saw another American aviator fly very low over the town, apparently looking for the disappeared aviator.

116

Signatures of the following inhabitants:

Perton	Leon Henry
Rene Colin	Cortlae Delbart
Auguste Cuny	Gabriel Didier
Henry Gustave	Camille Phillipe
Eugene Coline	Voliner Nicholas
Odile Patouche	Vallentine Garre
Richard Victor	Gustave Garre

The undersigned themselves placed the body of the aviator on the wagon and conducted it to the cemetery:

Cortlae Delbart, Voliner Nicholas

Seen for legalization of signatures placed above:

The Mayor, AUGUST GARRE,

Murvaux, Jan. 15, 1919.

[Seal of Murvaux]

The German version of Luke's death, never before published, is almost identical with the French.

Lieutenant B. Mangels, who after the war resided in Münster, commanded the balloon company controlling the last two balloons Luke vanquished, and directed the machine-gun fire that gave Frank his death wound.

For some time there was a controversy between Lieutenant Mangels and Lieutenant G. Roesch, who commanded an antiaircraft battery near the balloon; but Roesch has admitted that it was Mangels' machine gunners who brought the Balloon Buster down.

On September 29, one of Lieutenant Mangels' balloons was aloft northwest of Murvaux on the western slope of the Côte St. Germain. This was balloon Number Thirty-five of the Fifth German Army. A short distance away, over Brière Farm, hung balloon Number Sixty-four—the second bag Luke shot down on his last flight.

As Frank's plane dived for the third sausage, Mangels, who was on ground duty, personally directed a concentrated machine-gun fire against the Arizonian's plane and is certain he registered on the pilot's body.

Learning a few minutes later that Luke had crashed beyond Murvaux, Mangels hurried to the scene, but found Luke dead when he arrived. Mangels, the first officer to arrive, was able to identify the body as Luke's through an English citation, the finding of which he describes:

117

In his pockets we found a letter of appreciation from English Headquarters testifying that he had shot down nine balloons recently. Unfortunately, the great responsibility which weighed upon me in those days as the leader of a balloon company made it impossible for me to attend his funeral. His insignia I took and kept in remembrance of this great and fearless sportsman. He was a man of dazzling courage, one of the bravest we fought in the war.

When Captain Grant learned the details of Luke's last fight and his pistol battle with the enemy, he went immediately to Major Hartney.

"Luke ought to have the Congressional Medal of Honor," he told the Group Commander.

Grant was opposed to Luke's conduct from the standpoint of discipline, but he was the first to urge America's highest award for bravery for the flier he had ordered under arrest.

Of 1,390,000 American soldiers, sailors, and marines who actually saw battle service in France, only ninety received the Congressional Medal, and only four army aviators were so honored. Frank Luke was one of them.

Sixteen British army airmen received the coveted Victoria Cross, and France has even been criticized for her lavish bestowal of the Legion of Honor. There is scarcely an aviator who saw air-battle service under the French who does not wear the red ribbon of the Legion.

The very requirements necessary for eligibility to the Congressional Medal—namely: "conspicuous gallantry and intrepidity above and beyond the call of duty"—make it almost impossible for a pilot to win the decoration. Air combat, bombing operations, balloon strafing are a fighting pilot's allotted tasks, and the Congressional Medal is only for those capable of greater achievements.

Despite the exacting qualifications required of those who would be numbered among America's superheroes, there could be no doubt of Frank's eligibility after the story told by the peasants of Murvaux became known.

In due course, the medal was presented to Frank's father with this citation:

118

For conspicuous gallantry and intrepidity above and beyond the call of duty in action with the enemy near Murvaux, France, September 29, 1918. After having previously destroyed a number of enemy aircraft within seventeen days, he voluntarily started on a patrol after German observation balloons.

Though pursued by eight German planes, which were protecting the enemy balloon line, he unhesitatingly attacked and shot down in flames three German balloons, being himself under heavy fire from ground batteries and the hostile planes. Severely wounded, he descended to within fifty meters of the ground and, flying at this low altitude near the town of Murvaux, opened fire upon enemy troops, killing six and wounding as many more. Forced to make a landing and surrounded on all sides by the enemy, who called upon him to surrender, he drew his automatic pistol and defended himself gallantly until he fell dead from a wound in the chest.

There's a patron saint for you, you grinning young hellions upon whose youthful shoulders the rod of wartime discipline fell heavily. Glory in him, you easy-going buckaroos who sang unprintable songs while you thumbed your noses at the martinet's idol, Discipline! Glory in him— Frank Luke—the only man in the annals of the nation who ever won its greatest honor while under military arrest!

In addition to the Congressional Medal of Honor, there were the Distinguished Service Cross, the Italian War Cross, the Aëro Club Medal for Bravery, and the Margarita Fisher Gold Medal for the first Rockwell Field pilot to conquer an enemy in the air.

The Distinguished Service Cross with oak-leaf cluster, equivalent to two citations, was awarded for his earlier victories. The citation reads:

For extraordinary heroism in action near St. Mihiel, France, September 12-15, 1918. By skill, determination, and bravery, and in the face of heavy enemy fire, he successfully destroyed eight enemy observation balloons in four days. He is also awarded an oak-leaf cluster for the following act of extraordinary heroism near Etain, France, September 18, 1918:

Immediately after destroying two enemy observation balloons he was attacked by a large formation of German planes (type Fokker). He turned to attack two which were directly behind him and shot them down. Sighting an enemy plane (biplane,) although his gasoline was nearly gone, he attacked and destroyed this machine also.

He had won bronze for his chest, even beyond his dreams. There were other honors. As a further token of its appreciation, the United States Government named its Hawaiian flying field Luke Field, and in Phoenix a memorial arch was to be dedicated to him.

That is how he was regarded in Arizona, indeed in the entire Southwest—one of the mighty. It was not only by the younger generation that he was held in this high regard, but by the old-timers, too, who were proud of him.

Let me instance that by quoting Scott White.

Scott White, who ten years after Frank Luke's death was superintendent of the Arizona Penitentiary at Florence, was the type of old-timer who might have walked out of the pages of your favorite Western.

He was white-haired, but his eyes were sharp. He had served his apprenticeship as a peace officer as Sheriff of Cochise County when that county was hell-roaring country. In his day, Tombstone was tough and raucously proud of it. He helped "gentle" it so it stands without hitching—most of the time. I asked him what he thought of Frank Luke, and he stared at me, looking through and beyond me down the years to other fighters he had known. He spoke slowly.

"I guess," he said, "he was the gamest human I ever met. It's too bad we can't keep his kind."

But Frank Luke had to go. This plodding world of ours wasn't geared sufficiently high for him. Our wide spaces were too narrow, our precarious places too secure. He required the limitless paths of the stars, the breath-taking moments that come when death rides out, flanked by danger and disaster, and most men cower. Think of men concerned about the morning train to the office, worried over a change in the weather, or perturbed because of dollars they will never touch. Then think of Frank Luke.

120

You see? His kind has to go. We little people are in the majority, and the speed of things must be regulated to our needs.

Frank Luke couldn't find the even tempo of minor men. His was the quickstep of a regiment hurrying to bolster a sagging line. The pace of his horse was the clattering gallop of a needed battery changing ground. His pattern of life altered as swiftly as the ground under the Spad beside which he died.

That's about all there is to tell. No, there is this:

Frank Luke's father and I stood on the balcony of the Arizona Club in Phoenix, looking off across the twilight-shadowed Salt River Valley to the desert beyond, and the challenging buttes of the Superstition Mountains beyond that.

Ten years had passed since Frank Luke died. We had put in the day talking of his son, looking at old letters, touching reverently the things Frank had touched. Until then I had regarded Lieutenant Frank Luke, Jr. as a figure aloof, apart—as most of us regard people history has marked.

"You were willing to have Frank's body remain in France?" I asked.

"Yes," Frank's father said. "You see, when they took him to Romagne where those thousands of other boys are, it seemed right to leave him there. He would have wanted it, I know that, and I wanted to do the thing that would have pleased him most. But sometimes, when I'm alone and get to going over the old days, I wish—I can't help wanting—"

His voice broke, steadied, and he concluded:

"He was such a darn lively kid!"